Perfect Bound

How to Navigate the Book Publishing Process Like a Pro

To Mary Ann—
Keep 'em laughing!

Katherine Pickett

Katherine Pickett

HOP
ON
Publishing

ISBN 978-0-9914991-1-3 (paperback)
        978-0-9914991-2-0 (e-book)

Library of Congress Control Number: 2014907683

Cover and interior design by Suett Communications
Cover photograph copyright © iStock.com/Ryan Kelly

Hop On Publishing, LLC
P.O. Box 2794
Silver Spring, MD 20915
www.HopOnPublishing.com

Printed in the United States of America

To Chris, with love

Contents

7

Making It Real: Printers, Distributors, and E-Book Companies 143

8

Getting Used to Self-Promotion: Marketing and Publicity 167

Preface

I n my fifteen years in the publishing industry, I've edited some highly successful books, including Warren Phillips's *Newspaperman* (McGraw-Hill, 2011), Bill Neal's *Sex, Murder, and the Unwritten Law* (Texas Tech University Press, 2009), and Bill Walsh's *The Elephants of Style* (McGraw-Hill, 2004). Unfortunately, I have also seen plenty of good book ideas that were sunk by poor decisions.

Often the problem lay in a lack of planning on the part of the author: some authors had never considered how they would sell their book once it was completed. Other times it was a matter of authors not understanding what their role would be once they started on the road to publication. In both cases, the authors were unprepared for the challenges and work involved in creating and marketing a truly great product. Given the wealth of books and websites dedicated to writing and publishing, how could this be? With a little investigation I discovered the problem. Although there is an abundance of information on how to approach an agent, craft a novel, or produce an e-book in one day, few resources explain how the publishing process works, how to apply market research to your writing, and how those two factors relate to creating a book that succeeds in the marketplace.

More than anything, I hate to see wasted effort and wasted time. And I like to help. With my experience as a former in-house editor and now as a freelance copyeditor and proofreader, I am in a position to do that. That's why I began giving presentations to writing classes and publishers' associations. I have seen many sides of the book publishing process; I have edited more than three hundred books, and I know what needs to happen for a book to be successful. I was able to share that experience in my presentations.

Now I want to share that information with you. I want your book to succeed, too!

When I look back I realize I've been gathering the information for this book for more than a decade. I started my career in 1999 as an intern with NTC/Contemporary Publishing Group (before it was bought by the McGraw-Hill Companies a year later), working in the acquisitions department. As the assistant to an assistant editor, I was charged with sorting through the editor's slush pile. That's where I learned how acquisitions editors prioritize the submissions they receive. As I read through proposals, I was surprised by how many authors clearly had not researched our company to know what we published and how many others had not read the submission guidelines to know what to send. All that effort—and postage—to submit, say, a book of poetry to a company that hadn't published poetry in twenty years!

From the internship I moved into the production department as a project editor, where I guided manuscripts through editing and design and on to become a bound book. (E-books were just coming into their own when I was doing this work in the early 2000s.) Yet even here I saw books that simply missed the mark. Although their ideas were good, these authors had fallen victim to what I now think of as potholes—those mistakes that have the ability to slow down or sideline your book project if you don't know how to avoid them. I would work with the copyeditor, author, and proofreader to alleviate these issues as much as I could, but some problems can't be fixed that late in the process. Problems such as an unclear audience and a weak marketing hook go far deeper than any copyeditor can be expected to delve.

When I tried my hand at freelance copyediting and proofreading, I saw even rougher manuscripts and realized just what acquisitions editors are up against when they work with authors who do not know what they are getting into when they decide to publish a book. This lack of understanding was made ever more obvious when I began working with self-publishers in 2008. I was excited to see so many people who wanted to jump into publishing! There were so many passionate writers with solid concepts for a book. Yet, the success rate was low. In some cases the problem was basic: the idea for the book was never going to sell. But just as often, good ideas were doomed because the author had not done the background work necessary to put together a truly great book. I was often disappointed because what sounded like a strong, marketable idea that would add value to the field or genre, fell short.

There are also many technical aspects to publishing a book that I would spend hours explaining to my authors. Again, I was always happy to help—publishing is my passion, too—but I was supposed to be the copyeditor, not an instructor on the inner workings of book publishing. I felt we were wasting time and money at a point when we should be charging ahead. Those conversations became the basis for my series of workshops, "Sell Your Book!" and "Publish That Book!" as I decided it would be much easier if I could get a group of five or six writers together, sit down with them face-to-face, and explain everything one time. The writers gained from my experience as well as the collective knowledge of the group, and hosting those events was a truly rewarding experience for me. But by teaching five or six people at a time, I realized, I could never reach all the people who need this information. Plus, I couldn't get into all of the side topics, the details, and the ins and outs in the time allowed. What I needed was to write a book. And so I did.

Introduction

Publishing a book is a long road, and it is easy for the unsuspecting author to be waylaid at various points along that journey. Considerations like preparing a business plan, improving your knowledge of the market, and choosing the best route to publication can become lost in the shuffle when simply writing the book takes a thousand hours or more. The goal becomes typing "The End" on the last page of the manuscript, while thoughts of how to sell the book once it is completed—whether that is to agents, to publishers, or directly to readers—are pushed to the back of one's mind. When that happens, rather than creating a high-quality, highly marketable book that sells, aspiring writers may find themselves with a completed manuscript that no one will ever read.

The challenge to stay the course is even greater when authors don't know what to expect on the road to publication. Who will they be working with? What is it like to work with a designer? How does the acquisitions process work, and what do proofreaders do? All of these questions signal hidden potholes that can take a good book idea and send it bouncing off the road. Once that happens, it can require a lot of time, money, and effort for authors to get heading in the right direction again. Unfortunately, some authors discover the problem when it is too late to fix it. After years of work, their book is published to poor reviews and stalling sales. That terrible fate could have been avoided. What they needed was a guide to direct them around the obstacles. What they needed was *Perfect Bound: How to Navigate the Book Publishing Process Like a Pro.*

My intention with this book is not to teach you how to become a great writer. There are a multitude of critique groups, workshops, conferences, websites, and classes intended for that purpose, and I do believe they will guide you better than I can. In fact, I encourage you to research these opportunities in your area and get involved in the writing community. Hone your craft, because solid writing is essential to your success. But as I will say many times throughout this book, good writing is only one of the tools you will need as you endeavor to publish your book. You also need market savvy, professionalism, and drive. Only you can provide the drive. This book will help you improve your market savvy and professionalism so that you can create a book that sells.

Over the course of eight chapters, I guide you on the road from manuscript to completed book and introduce you to the many professionals who will be involved in your manuscript's transformation. Although fiction and nonfiction books have different needs, all manuscripts go through roughly the same steps to becoming published, and your role in the process is largely the same. From choosing your route to publication to acquisitions and manuscript development, through design and layout and on to printing, binding, and e-book conversion, each chapter of this book includes what you can expect, what is expected of you, and a step-by-step explanation of that stage of the publishing endeavor. At the end of each chapter I highlight the most common mistakes—the Potholes—that promise to delay you and cost you money, and I offer practical steps you can take to avoid them. Determining your audience, researching the competition, strengthening your marketing hook, and attending to research and permissions are all covered. Further, you will learn what to look for when you review your page proofs, how to use design to its greatest effect, what to include on your copyright page, and what you can do to move forward after rejection. Finally, in the last chapter I present some brief, practical guidance on how to get media exposure, how to use social media to promote your book, and how to make the most of your time online.

Throughout the book I offer case studies—highlights and lowlights from my career as an editor—along with interviews with nearly a dozen other authors and professionals in the field, so that you can learn from those who have gone before you. You will also find inside tips that can save you time and money, plus information on the various accommodations you have to make for books with special needs, such as those with a large art program, children's books, and academic titles. An annotated Resources section at the end guides you to selected books, websites, and organizations that will bolster your understanding of how to approach agents, write proposals, and market your book and will assist you throughout your publishing venture.

To get the most out of this book, I recommend reading it through completely one time while you are still writing your manuscript, before you embark on the book publishing process. The explanations of the Potholes and how to avoid them have been placed with the stage of production where they are most relevant, but even if you skip some of the production process, I encourage you to read all of the Potholes to ensure that you are not falling victim to one of these avoidable mistakes. Then, when you are ready to move ahead, return to the relevant chapters in this book as you make your own way through production so that you have the details of the process fresh in your mind. You will soon discover that when you know what to expect and what's expected of you, you save yourself considerable time, money, and embarrassment while at the same time making a high-quality, highly marketable book.

I have seen a lot of mistakes in my day, a lot of good book ideas that never made it. Will your book suffer the same fate or be a smashing success? With *Perfect Bound*, you have the advantage. Take it!

1

Choosing Your Route to Publication

One of your early considerations when planning to write a book is which path to take to get your book published. This is not a decision you have to make right away, and after you have read this book you will know better which route is right for you because you will understand what each path entails. Still, it is helpful to know your options up front so that you can begin thinking about them. In this chapter you'll discover the benefits and drawbacks of the two most common paths now available to writers, traditional and self-publishing, along with some of the lesser-known avenues to publication. How do you decide which route is best for you? You will find your greatest success when you follow the path that best complements your strengths and minimizes your weaknesses. And how do you know what your strengths and weaknesses are? The quiz at the start of this chapter will begin to illuminate your assets and limitations. Crafting a business plan, the subject of this chapter's first Pothole, will fill in the rest of the picture.

Hand in hand with developing a business plan is setting out a realistic schedule for yourself. Your choice of route may be strongly influenced by the time frame in which you wish to have your book published. The second

Every route to publication has its pros and cons. Consider what your own strengths and weaknesses are before choosing your path.

Pothole in this chapter offers some guidelines for budgeting your time at each stage of the book publishing process to ensure you have the time to create a high-quality book.

Ten Questions to Help You Choose Your Route

Each of the five routes to publication discussed in this chapter—traditional, self-publishing, collaborating with a nonprofit or business, work made for hire, and assisted self-publishing—requires certain assets of the author, whether it be money, a willingness to share creative control, or a marketing platform that can't be beat. Take this brief quiz to help you discover your assets and locate the path to publication that is right for you.

1. Do you have at least $5,000 you can dedicate to editing, designing, and marketing your book? ☐ Yes ☐ No

2. Do you want complete creative control over the text, layout, and cover? ☐ Yes ☐ No

3. Do you have unquestionable credentials, such as a degree or many years of experience in your field? ☐ Yes ☐ No

4. Do you have a narrow, targeted niche or cause? ☐ Yes ☐ No

5. Are you willing to give up some creative control in order to make a living as a writer? ☐ Yes ☐ No

6. Do you want a book under your name but would rather have someone else take care of the details of publication? ☐ Yes ☐ No

7. Do you have contacts, or are you willing to make contacts, with professionals who can help you publish a book on your own? ☐ Yes ☐ No

8. Do you have a book idea with widespread appeal? ☐ Yes ☐ No

9. Do you have a regional or national marketing platform already in place? ☐ Yes ☐ No

10. Do you want your book to be published in less than a year?

☐ Yes
☐ No

Now review the questions to which you answered yes. These are the assets you bring with you to the publishing endeavor. Use them to help you determine your route.

- ◆ If you answered yes to questions 1, 2, 7, 9, and 10, then self-publishing may be right for you. Self-publishing requires some initial capital but offers the greatest level of control in content and production.

- ◆ If you answered yes to questions 3, 4, 5, 8, and 9, traditional publishing may be right for you. Traditional publishing requires a fully developed marketing platform and a book project with regional or national appeal, but it does not require the initial monetary investment of self-publishing.

- ◆ If you answered yes to questions 3 and 4, collaboration with a nonprofit or business may be right for you. An alternative path for fiction and nonfiction writers, collaborations offer flexibility for those with a well-defined niche or cause, with the caveat that your reach may be narrow.

- ◆ If you answered yes to questions 5, 6, and 8, work made for hire may be right for you. For professional writers, avoiding the nitty-gritty of book production tasks means more time for writing.

- ◆ If you answered yes to questions 6 and 10, then assisted self-publishing may be right for you. Assisted self-publishing offers a fast turnaround and minimal involvement in the logistics of book production, but it requires a monetary investment from the author. *Thoroughly research the self-publishing company you choose before following this path.*

You will notice that there is some overlap with each category. For most authors, there is more than one right way to publish a book. Your own goals for your book will also factor into your decision.

With the results of this quiz, however, you are ready to explore the options most suited to you. Keep your answers in mind as you read the rest of this chapter.

THE GOOD AND BAD ON PUBLISHING HOUSES

For many writers, getting picked up by a major publishing house is the ultimate dream—and that's understandable. Much prestige comes from being associated with the likes of Random House or HarperCollins. Sporting the logo of a midsize publisher, such as Houghton Mifflin Harcourt, John Wiley, or Hyperion, is nothing to scoff at either. For writers of academic works, publishers such as University of Chicago Press or University of California Press have their own glow of prestige. But any choice for partnership in publishing comes with pros and cons. Let's start with the benefits before we discuss the drawbacks.

What's in It for You

As mentioned, one of the biggest perks of signing with a publishing house is the prestige that comes with it. There is no stigma to having a St. Martin's Press logo on the spine of your book, as there can be with a self-published book. You will also receive a monetary advance—a portion when you sign the contract and another when your manuscript is accepted—a benefit not offered by some of the other routes to publication. The size of this advance depends a great deal on the book you are writing, your credentials, whether or not an agent is involved, and who is publishing it. A realistic advance for a first-time author is between $2,000 and $10,000, although much larger advances—up to the $500,000 range—are possible, even for debut authors. A larger publishing house will have more money to spend on you than a midsize or academic press will, but as we'll see in the next section, there are always trade-offs.

Another perk to traditional publishing is the sharing of the responsibility, the costs, and the risks. The publishing house will coordinate the entire production process, hiring professional editors, designers, marketers, printers and binders, and distributors. You still have a role in the process, but the house will arrange and pay for the services of these vendors. Marketing responsibilities will also be shared, with the publisher arranging press releases and other marketing materials while you provide many of the connections for local media appearances and the like.

Traditional publishers, with their many years in the field, also have an expertise that the average person does not have. A surprising number of conventions are intrinsic to bookmaking, and while many of these go unnoticed when they are done correctly, when done *incorrectly* it shows. Did you know you should never have a blank right page? Have you noticed there are never running heads on a chapter opener? Do you know the tricks to reaching your ideal page count or ensuring the spine of your book is wide enough so that the title is legible? These are just a few of the polished touches that make it clear when a professional has taken care of the details. You can certainly learn these concepts as you go, but there is no learning curve for traditional publishers.

Further, your publishing house will have connections in the industry that you do not. This relates not only to the vendors that will be hired to help produce your book but also to the distributors, bookstores, and media outlets. Barnes and Noble will not turn its nose up when Perseus Books approaches with a new book. Printers are more likely to make room for a large book publisher compared to an individual with a very short print run. And with fifty to one hundred years of experience in the book industry, a traditional press will undoubtedly be able to get special treatment and deals that aren't available to the general public.

What You Give Up

One word sums up what you miss when you contract with a publishing house: control. Although you will have a say in most aspects of your book project, you may feel pushed aside or even ignored when it comes to the decisions you cannot make.

To start, particularly if you are writing nonfiction, your creative control is limited. Initially you may find yourself arguing with your acquisitions editor about the direction your manuscript should take. If you like to tell a meandering story with side trails and tangents, it is likely your editor will try to rein you in. Perhaps you envisioned your book with a dual focus, say, part memoir, part self-help; it's possible your editor will attempt to steer you in one direction or the other. Ideally this discussion is held before you sign a contract, in which case you can walk away from the deal with no harm done. But if you have signed a contract and accepted the first portion of your advance, you may be in a sticky situation.

You may also find that you do not like the copyeditor or designer that the publishing house has arranged. You have recourse in this case, but particularly with regard to design, your input and creative control will be significantly limited. Further, the marketing budget for your book may be small or nonexistent, you may be asked to do more of the marketing chores than you anticipated, or your first print run (that is, the number of books printed when your book first publishes) may be considerably smaller than the six million J.K. Rowling famously received or even the modest five thousand you were hoping for. That makes it a lot harder to meet the royalty thresholds you agreed to in your contract. Which leads to the next point. To go along with the shared responsibilities mentioned in the previous section, you must also share the profits, and, as they say, the odds are on the house. A common royalty structure is 10 percent of the cover price for the first 5,000 books sold, 12.5 percent for 5,000–10,000 books, and 15 percent for 10,000 and above. That's a lot of books to sell, and, depending on your cover price, it may mean less than a dollar in your pocket per

> **Inside Tip**
>
> Royalty structures can vary dramatically. Some publishers pay royalties on the cover price, the best scenario for authors. Others pay on the net price. The net price is the price at which the publisher sells the book to wholesalers and retailers, or about 45 percent of the cover price. Also, royalty rates change depending on the format of the book; hardcover books and e-books tend to pay higher rates than paperbacks. If you wish to sign with a traditional publisher, read your contract carefully to ensure you understand how you will be paid.

unit sold. And don't forget, you have to earn back that advance before royalties begin to accrue. Many authors never do earn back their full advance and therefore never earn royalties. Writing, to be sure, is not a get-rich-quick scheme.

Last but not least, one major downside to working with a publishing house is getting noticed by the house in the first place. Publishing houses are gatekeepers, and they decide who is worthy of publication under their imprints. Persistence is key, but it can take many months to find a publisher. And if you don't want to wait the additional eighteen months to two years that it often takes to have your book hit the market after it has been accepted, this may not be the route for you.

ROADSIDE ASSISTANT

Judy Lewin
Author and genealogist

When it comes to deciding a route to publication, many authors may feel that they don't have a choice. Judy Lewin tells a different story. Although her manuscript for *Forensic Genealogist Solves a Family Mystery After 50 Years* drew serious interest from a traditional publisher, Judy withdrew from the negotiations. After hearing the publisher's suggestions to significantly change the book, she decided to continue searching for a publisher that supported her vision. Judy's credits include awards for writing, solving a genealogy puzzle, and bringing two brothers together. "This has been thrilling and I want the world to know!" Judy says.

After your experience, what did you learn about traditional publishing versus self-publishing?
Traditional publishers are in a business to earn a profit, while self-publishing may not necessarily be for profit. The author may only want one copy of a book in print. On many levels, holding a "proof" copy of my book with my name and my bio on the back cover is my reward.

How did you make your decision to withdraw from the traditional publisher?

I made my decision to withdraw from a contract offered by a traditional publisher because I was afraid, and I was afraid to give up control of my story and writing. My complex and true story, *Forensic Genealogist Solves a Family Mystery After 50 Years*, is an accomplishment: I found a missing person, my husband's mother, without knowing her correct name, date of birth, or last known address. I had been looking for Mary Lewin, but she never existed! My first clue was when I learned her name was Mary Brown.

The publisher asked me to "sign away the editing of my book" and wanted to focus the story on a happy ending, when my husband finds his mother's grave and his younger brother, who was living less than fifty miles from our home. I agreed, but I also wanted to tell the entire story of my husband's mother's agony, the deceit, cover-up, and crimes committed along the way. The publisher did not agree with me.

What advice do you have for new authors regarding choosing a route to publication?

Decide what you want. I want to be in the bestselling nonfiction category for my true story and may need to work with a traditional publisher. For now, I am self-publishing fiction to get experience and learn how to rewrite, rewrite, rewrite. A good story and good editing will lead to my success.

What are your thoughts on dealing with rejection?

I am crushed when the rejection letters come. However, every rejection means I am that much closer to acceptance.

THE PROMISE AND PERILS OF SELF-PUBLISHING

After traditional publishing, the next most common avenue to publication is self-publishing. Today more than ever before, self-publishing, also called indie publishing, is a practical, straightforward way to get your book into the hands of your readers. In fact, according to a 2012 press release from R.R. Bowker, the official ISBN agency for the United States, "The number of self-published books produced annually in the U.S. has nearly tripled, growing 287 percent since 2006, and now tallies more than 235,000 print and 'e' titles [e-books]." Of course, there are upsides and downsides here as well, and you should know what you're getting into before you invest in self-publishing your book.

What's in It for You

The stigma of self-publishing is quickly vanishing as more and more self-published authors reach the *New York Times* bestseller list and are picked up by major publishers for significant advances. Even some of the big-name traditionally published authors are taking to self-publishing for their latest projects. The quality of these books is also increasing, and, with today's technology, it is more than possible for a self-published book to compete with and look respectable next to the traditionally published books that share the space on bookshelves and in online bookstores.

As the inverse of traditional publishing, self-publishing gives the author complete control. You can write your manuscript in whatever manner you wish. If it makes more sense to you to have a dual focus for your book, or to take side trails in the narrative, you are free and able to publish your book that way. Even if someone else questions your approach, it is ultimately your decision—you are the publisher. Creativity is welcome and encouraged.

You also have complete control over who makes up your publishing team. You will hire the copyeditor and designer. You will arrange the printing and binding or conversion to an e-book. It is your choice whether to hire a marketing expert or perform those tasks yourself, and distribution is also yours to manage. In this way you are assured that you will be working with people who understand your vision and support you.

Perhaps an even more appealing aspect to self-publishing is that you are able to keep the profits. There is no advance, but neither is there a royalty split that requires selling more than 10,000 copies just to earn 15 percent of the cover price. Your earnings begin as soon as you sell your first copy.

And finally, there are no gatekeepers to self-publishing except the readers themselves. If you have the desire and the drive to publish your work, you can. And you can do it in any format, at any cost you choose. In the end you will have accomplished something significant and achieved your dream of publication.

What You Give Up

After reading the preceding section, you may wonder why anyone would *not* choose self-publishing. Well, there are a few reasons. One factor that keeps many writers from self-publishing is how overwhelming it can be to take on all of the responsibilities of a publisher. Self-publishers must manage every aspect of bookmaking and marketing, and there can be a pretty steep learning curve. *Perfect Bound* will help, but the amount of work involved is a definite consideration.

Another factor is the expense. As publisher you carry all of the reward . . . and all of the risk. To create a high-quality book that sells, you need to hire a professional copyeditor and a designer, at the very least. You may also use a proofreader, indexer, printer and binder, and distributor. If you opt for an e-book, you have the associated fees of an e-book company. Marketing materials, if professionally done, can be expensive; if done yourself, you need to factor in your time as an expense. As I explain more fully in the coming chapters, these services combined can total $5,000 to $10,000, depending on the length and complexity of the manuscript, and more if you need to hire an illustrator or photographer. (Some authors spend as much as $50,000 to publish their books, although this is likely money *not* well spent.) And remember, this money is coming out of your pocket. You don't have an advance to lean on.

Further, the money you receive per unit sold, although greater than what you would get from a publishing house, is generally not the price you have listed on your cover. Should people buy your book directly from you, then all of the money accrues to you. But if you sell through a bookstore, the bookseller will expect a

55 percent discount. That means for a $10 book, you get $4.50. E-books sold through Amazon generally have a better structure, with Amazon taking only 30 percent for books priced between $2.99 and $9.99. They take 65 percent for books priced above or below that range. And you need to consider how many books you would have to sell to earn back that $5,000 to $10,000 you put in. This fact alone explains one barrier to self-publishing and why it is a good idea to prepare a business plan before writing your manuscript. With that kind of investment, it's best to know just how you're going to break even, much less make a profit.

Related to the money issue is the ability to find respectable vendors to work with. You are able to build your own team, but do you know whom to hire? Do you know where to find them? Can you ensure that you are getting the best deal possible? And how are you going to reach your target market without connections to the major bookstores? This book will answer many of those questions, but making the right contacts is a hurdle that authors who sign with a traditional publisher will not face. For those who already have contacts or are willing to go out and get them, and who aren't afraid to put in some elbow grease, self-publishing becomes a much more viable option.

OTHER AVENUES TO PUBLICATION

We have covered the two most common ways of getting your book out into the world. Now let's look at some of the less talked-about avenues to publication: collaborating with nonprofits and businesses, works made for hire, and assisted self-publishing.

Collaborating with Nonprofits and Businesses

Collaboration with nonprofits and businesses as a means to publication may be best suited to nonfiction writers, but the right fiction book can also be appealing to certain entities. A collaboration requires making contacts with an appropriate nonprofit organization or business and arranging to either copublish or have the organization publish your book, with you as author. You may be familiar with this kind of book if you have purchased books published through a museum, historical society, or other cause-driven association.

What's in It for You

You often don't need an agent for this avenue of publishing. Instead, you can approach the organization or business directly with your proposal and work out a contract yourselves. (One caveat: If you go without an agent, I would encourage you to have a literary lawyer review the contract before signing away your rights.) Depending on your specific agreement, you may be in charge of the writing while the partnering organization or business takes care of artwork and the hiring of vendors. You are generally dealing with a group that already has a publication department, so you can rely on their expertise to get the manuscript published the best way possible. Contracts will vary, but you may opt to forgo an advance in favor of a higher royalty structure. In all, the greatest benefit here is flexibility. You can make this arrangement however suits you and the partnering organization best. And if you find the right partner, you have an immediate "in" with your target audience, combined with the respectability of the organization you have teamed with.

What You Give Up

While you gain flexibility in the kind of agreement you are signing, you are restricted to the nonprofits and businesses that are both interested in your topic and already have a publication department. (You'll have a much harder time convincing an organization without a publication department to take on this kind of project.) Further, your manuscript will need to fit within a much smaller niche for it to make sense to the organization to collaborate with you. The Muscular Dystrophy Association, for example, would not be inclined to invest time and money in a book that does not directly deal with MD.

Another consideration is finances. You may be asked to share in the cost of publication, including marketing and production expenses, as a trade-off for the potentially higher royalty rate you would receive. This is a compromise you will have to consider closely before signing a contract. If you don't have the capital, it may not be feasible to go this route.

And finally, the reach of such an organization, whether a business or a nonprofit, may be limited when compared to a full-fledged publishing house. Your manuscript will be written with a narrow market in mind, and that is who will have the most access to your book. Nevertheless, if you have the right book and find the right organization, this is an excellent option for those authors who are looking for flexibility but are not so concerned with publishing a bestseller.

Works Made for Hire

A work made for hire is a creative work performed under the terms of a contract. Any organization or group can commission and publish a work made for hire, but if you are a book author, you will most likely want to look for a traditional publisher. However, this route to publication is a little different from what normally comes to mind when you think of traditional publishing. Work-for-hire agreements entail proposing a book (often as part of an established series), writing the book, and then selling it for a one-time fee to the publisher. For full-time writers, this can be their bread and butter. For first-time authors, this may be a nice way to learn the ropes and earn a byline to add to your résumé. Although this may be best suited to nonfiction writers, genre fiction writers (for example, romance and fantasy writers) can also find opportunities in this area.

What's in It for You

Works made for hire are desirable because they can mean a steady and reliable source of income. You or your agent may approach the publishing house initially, but if you build a solid relationship with an editor there, the house may begin contacting you when they need to fill a certain hole in a series. You usually write on subjects you enjoy, and you can learn about a variety of topics that you may otherwise not be introduced to. Most often your pay is not dependent on the number of books sold, as you get an up-front fee in place of royalties, and you can more or less write the book and then forget it. Publishing, printing, and marketing the book are all taken care of by the publisher. You are responsible for submitting a manuscript that meets the requirements laid out in the agreement, and that's about it. For full-time writers, this is great news because it means they can move on to the next project without worry.

What You Give Up

The downsides of such a simple publishing model include a lack of creative control and limited earnings. You are generally writing to a specific construct and are expected to follow the style set out by other books in the series for which you are writing. Think of the ubiquitous Dummies series. All of the Dummies books have the same cover design and the same or similar interior layout, which means no money was required for new designs; they are low-cost, steady-return books for the publisher. And the author simply writes the material specific to whatever topic is chosen. Some series even have stock material for the first several chapters and then use the tailored material for the latter portions of the book. That means you don't have a lot of leeway for creativity—some, but not a lot.

Given the limited amount of work and risk demanded of the author, it's not a wonder that the pay is minimal. When I started working on such books as an editor in the early 2000s, the going rate was $500 for a 160-page book. A couple of years later it was up to $1,000. Today, $2,000 to $3,000 is reasonable.

You will also gain no fame or prestige from most works made for hire. The selling point for the reader is the established series, not the individual who wrote a particular book. Instead, you have a credit to your name, experience under your belt, and a potential relationship to keep the revenue stream going. For many aspiring authors, this type of work is a building block or a safety net, not a passion.

Assisted Self-Publishing

Although the previous two avenues to publication were more geared toward nonfiction writers, this final category is available to all writers and tends to be most appealing to memoirists and novelists. There are several models that can fall into this category. In one, the company provides editorial and design services, then carries your book through the full production process. Some companies take that a step further and market your book under their imprint. Often, each piece is charged a la carte, so that editing has one associated fee, design and layout another fee, marketing yet another. These companies often refer to themselves as self-publishers, but that is a bit of a misnomer. Their purpose is to help you through the process of self-publishing your book. Unfortunately, this model attracts a lot of sharks, and many of these companies prey on uneducated authors to purchase more than they need. Researching the company you hire and being your own advocate are two key lessons if you opt for this route. Two websites in particular, Preditors and Editors (www.pred-ed.com) and Science Fiction and Fantasy Writers of America (www.sfwa.org), offer excellent guidance for choosing a respectable company.

What's in It for You

The benefits of using one of these companies are that you still maintain your creative control over the manuscript, yet you do not have to arrange the vendors. You pay the company a set amount of money based on the length of your manuscript and the package you choose, and the company guides your book through the publishing process. Everything is done more or less on your schedule, and you are able to make or not make any of the changes that your copyeditor or proofreader suggests. With some companies, you also have the benefit of one of the company's logos on the spine of your book. That can go a long way in establishing credibility with consumers.

What You Give Up

Although this setup may sound ideal, if you aren't with the right company, it can be the worst of both worlds. As you would with do-it-yourself self-publishing, you put forth the capital, but then you give up control over your publishing team. For instance, your book may be assigned to a good copyeditor with many years of experience, or it may go to someone who is just starting out and who makes a lot of mistakes. You have no way of knowing ahead of time and no say in who is hired, yet you have to foot the bill.

One major benefit of working with a professional copyeditor is that the editor will save you from yourself; if you are making major errors of judgment, your editor will alert you to the problem and give you a chance to fix it. In assisted self-publishing, where you are not in direct contact with the copyeditor yet the copyeditor knows you hold the final decision-making power, he or she is more likely to chalk up any poor decisions to "author's preference" and not question you. You might think this would happen in traditional publishing also, where you often do not communicate with the copyeditor directly, but in that instance an in-house editor checks the copyediting for quality. With regular old DIY self-publishing, there is open communication between the copyeditor and the author, eliminating the tendency to assume certain "errors" were done intentionally. Those safety nets are missing with assisted self-publishing.

Furthermore, for both editors and designers, these companies often pay much less than what a publishing house pays, and, in the publishing industry, you really do get what you pay for. Even if the copyeditor or designer is normally very good at his or her job, projects that don't pay well may not receive the same level of attention as other, better-paying jobs. Although there is a chance of receiving this substandard treatment whenever you work with vendors, the odds are much greater with assisted self-publishing. The pay and the ethics of many of these companies attract some of the worst vendors. You will also have a hard time finding a company with truly good customer service when a problem does arise.

Most troubling, it seems a significant number of these companies are out to take advantage of the uneducated author. They use high-pressure tactics to get you to buy a more expensive package but don't tell you what's *not* included. When you have questions about the process, you get double-talk or you are unable to reach anyone at all. They take your money and give you nothing in return. If you are considering this path to publication, do a thorough vetting of the company: ask other writers about their experiences, look for reviews online, and keep your eyes peeled for any red flags. You must be your own advocate. While there are good companies out there, in the end, the best I can say about assisted self-publishing is, buyer beware.

— — — — — —

Many factors have to be considered when you choose your route to publication. Although some writers know immediately how they wish to be published, being aware of your options will ensure you are not closing doors prematurely. And while you may be emotionally attached to one path over another, considering all that is required of you and all that you bring to the table—your strengths and weaknesses—will help you select the route that leads to your success.

AVOIDING THE POTHOLE
Prepare a Book Business Plan

As you decide which path you wish to take to get your book published, you will benefit greatly from assessing your strengths and weaknesses and evaluating what your goals are. A book business plan can help.

The business plan has other benefits as well. It will help you answer the crucial question, how are you going to sell this book once it's completed? A plan that outlines who your target market is, who your competition is, and what your outlets are for selling the book will give your manuscript, and the publishing endeavor as a whole, direction. You will also be able to apply your findings to your writing so that you know you are crafting the most marketable book possible.

As you begin to draft your business plan, you must ask yourself a few essential questions. First, is this book idea truly one that people will buy? Second, is it worth the time, effort, and money it will take to get it published? Are you the best person to write this book, and do you have the stamina to get you through? This is what acquisitions editors, agents, and publishers want and need to know before taking on a project, and you, as author or author/publisher, should be just as discerning.

If you are putting together your business plan before or while writing your manuscript, you have put yourself in a great position. You have the opportunity to revamp your book idea before you spend a lot of time—or a lot *more* time—writing a book that is not going to sell. Furthermore, you will be able to select which route to publication to pursue that much sooner. Initially the document will be for your eyes only. However, those who wish to engage an agent or publisher can parlay the business plan into their book proposal and query letter, while all writers will gain invaluable insights into their book and the market in which they wish to pub-

lish. A realistic budget should accompany your business plan and will help you determine the areas where you may need to cut costs and where you should focus your spending. For self-publishers, a budget is a must if you wish at least to break even.

The Potholes in Chapters 2 and 3 delve much more deeply into the world (or abyss, if you prefer) of defining your target market, researching your competition, and developing a marketing hook, three major elements of a book business plan and essential information for you when you are communicating with publishing professionals and selling your book. Here we look briefly at the remaining pieces of the plan with an eye toward how these factors make your book more marketable. When you have completed your plan, you can assess your strengths and weaknesses to help you decide your most appropriate route to publication.

AUTHOR BACKGROUND AND PUBLICATION HISTORY

What makes you qualified to write your book? A compelling answer to this question is essential in selling your book to agents as well as readers. You are part of the marketing package, and your credentials strengthen your marketing platform. Particularly if you are writing nonfiction, you should outline your credentials and relate them to your manuscript. If you aren't an academic, in which case a degree in your area of study and publication in academic journals make up your credentials, your qualifications may include research you have done on your own, the organizations you belong to, and the life and career experience you have with your topic. Note any public speaking you have done, workshops you have held, classes you have taken, and brushes with fame you have had. Take a broad view of your experience to uncover all of your credentials.

Closely related to your qualifications as an author is your publication history. For fiction authors, previous publications often outweigh other credentials. Although it may help if you are a writing instructor at a prestigious college, more often it is the quality of your other published works, combined with strong writing skills, that gets you noticed. The more prestigious your previous publications, the more appealing you become to an agent, a publisher, and readers. Being published indicates three things: (1) someone else thought your work was worth publishing, (2) you may already have a fan base, and (3) you have some understanding of the publishing process. These are all very desirable aspects. For new authors, however, providing a publication history can be tricky. What do you say if you are writing your first book? If you have been keeping a blog and you have a significant number of followers, note that in your business plan. If you have had essays or stories accepted by online or print magazines, include that. And if you have never had anything else published, say so. This should be an honest evaluation of your assets as an author.

Having less than stellar credentials is not new, and it doesn't have to be the end of your attempt at successful publication. "One way to give yourself credibility is to get an expert to work with you," suggests Blythe Camenson, the author of *How to Sell, Then Write Your Nonfiction Book*. This collaboration can be as simple as asking an expert to contribute a foreword or as involved as having the expert work with you as a coauthor. With an expert's name attached to yours, you have more than doubled your credentials.

Now, if you find your background is lacking even after you've delved deep into your soul to find qualifications, you may want to take some time to build your credentials. Join organizations relevant to your writing topic or genre. Get involved with the community of people interested in what you write about by attending conferences, volunteering, or finding an appropriate meet-up group where you can interact with like-minded individuals. Also look for other opportunities for publication, whether that's submitting short stories and poems to journals, contributing articles and essays to relevant newsletters and magazines, or guest blogging for a blog in your field. Bobbi Linkemer, book coach, ghostwriter, writing instructor, and author of *How to Write a Nonfiction Book: From Planning to Promotion in 6 Steps*, advises

her students, "Don't make a book the first thing you ever write." That may sound obvious, but it's good advice for reasons other than to help you get published. Publishing is a long road. You need experience to fall back on if you are going to see your book project to the end. So get to writing. Seek publication. And whatever you do, grow your résumé!

MARKETING AND PUBLICITY OUTLETS

In traditional publishing, agents and publishers want to know how you are going to help them sell your book. In self-publishing, your marketing and publicity outlets are just as critical. These make up the avenues you will use to reach your readers and sell your book.

What constitutes a marketing outlet? Anything that gets you in touch with your audience. Do you conduct workshops, maintain a mailing list, or otherwise have access to your target market? Think creatively about whom and what you can leverage to help get your book in the hands of readers.

If you have not done so already, you must find the groups, organizations, and conferences that fit your niche, and join them. The members of these groups are your target market, and being involved with that community creates a marketing outlet. If you don't know where to find relevant groups, a quick search online will prove that there is an organization, association, foundation, meet-up, or other group for nearly everything imaginable. If somehow you have discovered that your topic area is not covered by such a group—say, those interested in growing flaxseed in their own backyard—form one. What better credential for an author of a book on flaxseed than to be the founder and president of the Maryland Flaxseed Growers Association?

Also take stock of which publications would be interested in reviewing your book and any people with name recognition who would be willing to attach themselves to your book via a quote or a foreword. Such opportunities for publicity make it possible for you to reach your readers.

FORMAT

What format your book takes relates directly to your ultimate vision for the book, that is, how it will look when you are finished. Having a clear vision for your book will keep you on track throughout the long publication process. So consider the following: What is the page count you have in mind? Do you see this as paperback or hardcover or e-book? Will there be illustrations or other artwork? Will the interior be color or black and white? What trim size are you envisioning? Realize that you might not get all of your wishes, but it is important to have a plan. Dream big!

As you go to answer these questions, think about what is currently on the market. While we all want our book to stand out on the store shelf, readers expect a certain amount of conformity. Self-help books need sidebars and helpful tips. Children's fiction requires a certain page length and artwork, depending on age range. Different kinds of adult fiction usually fall into just a couple of trim sizes and a small range of page counts. Scott Norton, in his book *Developmental Editing*, writes, "A book's success also rests largely on whether it conforms to the market's expectations regarding length, tone, depth of coverage, and the inclusion of key features." That means, to sell books, you have to give readers what they want and what they expect. You will need to research your competition to learn more about what content and other considerations your readers are looking for. The Potholes in Chapter 2 will help you.

It is also important to keep in mind what makes a book expensive, which is a potential turnoff to publishers and an important consideration for self-publishers, who will be putting forth the money for the entire book project. Paperback is cheaper than hardcover; black-and-white illustrations are cheaper than color. A shorter book will be less expensive at every stage, so if it's appropriate for your book and the market, aim for shorter rather than longer. Your acknowledgment of these facts in your business plan will show you understand that publishing is a business. Publishing a book on your own can easily run from $5,000 to $10,000, often more. If budget is a concern or you aren't sure how much of your investment you can expect to recoup, you may need to dream a little smaller.

ARTWORK OR OTHER SUPPLEMENTARY MATERIALS

First, let's define *artwork*. We are not talking fine arts here, necessarily. In publishing, any illustration, graph, chart, line drawing, or photograph is called art. In this section of your business plan, answer the following questions: What artwork, if any, will your book require? Do you have an artist already lined up? Do you have the artwork in hand? Will graphs and charts need to be created? Do you have licensing and permissions taken care of?

Why do you need to take these questions into account? Although artwork adds value to a book and may be virtually required in some types of works, books with artwork also cost more to produce. Hiring an artist or photographer and licensing artwork can add significant costs. If the artwork is four-color (that's lingo for what the rest of the world calls color), then special paper may need to be ordered to ensure quality printing, an additional cost. Keeping track of the artwork, pairing images with captions, and ensuring that files meet print-quality requirements add another layer of complexity. And complexity means more cost. Self-publishers need to have a firm grasp on their budgets and know where the expenses are adding up, and with publishing houses new authors need to justify the additional cost or offset it with their own investment.

> **Inside Tip**
>
> One alternative to a full art program that is becoming more and more popular is the insert. A happy compromise on cost and readers' expectations for photographs, an insert is the eight or sixteen pages of color or black-and-white photographs you see dropped in the middle of a book. This feature is cheaper than having photos placed throughout the book because you have to pay for only a few sheets of specialty paper, and you still get to have your photos. Perhaps an insert makes sense for your book.

THE BUDGET

Whether you are self-publishing, are looking for a publisher, or are undecided, you need to have a firm handle on how much of an investment your book project is going to be. Throughout *Perfect Bound* I offer some basic guidelines on how much the production of a book costs. Many variables come into play, specifically length, complexity, and genre, but even a rough estimate will be informative.

When you create your budget, consider both large and small items. The small items, such as head shots, writers conferences, and time with a literary attorney, can easily add up to $1,000. Self-publishers will also have to pay for some or all of the following: ISBNs, bar codes, marketing materials, specialty artwork, plus editing and design expenses. Be sure to add in travel expenses, the cost of a book launch if you will have one, and administrative costs as well. Total your expenses and then compare this number to what you expect to earn from your book. Remember that the list price is not how much you will make on each book; you must factor in a 40 to 55 percent discount. Often, books are not money makers. That need not deter you, but you do need to be grounded in reality when taking on the challenge of authorship.

— — — — — —

Much, much more could be said (and has been said) on this topic. I encourage you to explore the resources at the end of this book to learn more. Crafting a realistic business plan will take time and effort on your part, yet the information you glean by performing this exercise will inform your writing and your marketing, and it will help you choose the best path to publication, significantly increasing your chances for success.

AVOIDING THE POTHOLE
Build Enough Time into Your Publishing Schedule

Much of this chapter is about planning, and knowing how long it takes to make a book is an important part of that planning. To create a quality book and avoid unneeded frustration, you must build enough time into your schedule to allow the publishing professionals you work with to do a good job.

So how long does it take to publish a book? The following time line offers some guidance. Where you join the time line will depend on several factors, most notably, which publishing path you have chosen. Your personal goal for a publication date may help you choose that route.

Querying agents	3–12 months
Negotiating/signing with an agent	1–2 months
Querying publishers	3–12 months
Negotiating/signing with a publisher	2–4 months
Developmental editing	2–6 months
Copyediting	3 weeks–2 months
Query resolution	2–4 weeks
Design and layout	4–8 weeks (overlaps with query resolution)
Proofreading and author review	2–4 weeks
Revised proofs	2–4 weeks
Indexing	1–2 weeks
Printing and binding	1 month
E-book conversion	24 hours–1 week
Lead time for professional reviews	3–4 months

What if you don't allow enough time for your publication journey? A few things can happen. If you choose to keep your aggressive schedule, either you will pay more for a rush job or quality will suffer, or both. If by choice or necessity your schedule is blown and you miss your ideal publication date, you may lose out on prime marketing opportunities or the chance at professional reviews. Set a realistic schedule for your book to save yourself time and money and to ensure that you are producing the highest-quality book you can.

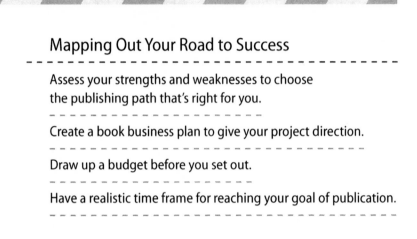

Mapping Out Your Road to Success

Assess your strengths and weaknesses to choose the publishing path that's right for you.

Create a book business plan to give your project direction.

Draw up a budget before you set out.

Have a realistic time frame for reaching your goal of publication.

2

Being Accepted
The Acquisitions Process

You often hear that agents have "contacts" with publishers. They *know people*, the mysterious gatekeepers, the ones who thus far have been keeping your book from being published. Who are these contacts who wield such great power? They are the acquisitions editors, those professionals who are tasked with bringing books into the publishing house.

Acquisitions editors (also called acquiring editors, AEs, or sponsoring editors) are one type of editor that self-publishers will never interact with. They are part of the editorial department inside a publishing house, and they generally report to the publisher. For those going the traditional route, AEs are an author's first contact with a publishing house and will remain a part of the book team throughout the production process and beyond.

If the author has signed with an agent, the AE will work with that agent throughout the negotiations that make up the acquisitions process. Authors who send their queries and proposals directly to the acquisitions editor will negotiate the terms of the publishing contract themselves. This chapter details the acquisitions process from the point when an AE has shown interest in a project.

Acquisitions editors are your advocates within the publishing house. Employ patience and trust to maintain a good working relationship.

TO SIGN OR NOT TO SIGN WITH AN AGENT

"Do I need an agent?" I hear this question frequently from aspiring authors, many times with a tinge of fear in their voices that I might say yes. Agents mean having an expert on your side to get you noticed and to assist with negotiations. But they also mean adding one more gatekeeper to the mix. Can't you get your book published without one? That depends on which publishing route you choose, which genre you write in, and which publisher you approach. Nonfiction writers have a slightly easier time getting a publisher without an agent than fiction writers; if you are writing fiction, you will almost certainly need an agent if you want to go through a publishing house.

While some university presses and small publishing houses are open to unagented manuscripts, they are becoming fewer and farther between. The so-called Big Five publishing houses—which include Hatchette, HarperCollins, Penguin Random House, Macmillan, and Simon and Schuster—don't accept anything without an agent. Each of these companies owns a dozen or more imprints that have their pick of books to pursue, and agents serve as a filter for the thousands of books that are submitted to them.

But what if you don't want to work with an agent? You're determined to find that small press that is willing to work with you as an individual. You don't want to add the six months or a year that it can take to find an agent before you even reach a publisher, and you don't know what the point of an agent is anyway. You are going to approach publishers directly. This is a viable option, and one that has worked well for many authors. But before you rule out agents entirely, you should know what signing with an agent means for you. "Generally speaking, an agented project will be picked up or rejected by most publishers within two to three weeks of submission," write Susan Rabiner and Alfred Fortunato, authors of *Thinking Like Your Editor: How to Write Great Serious Nonfiction—and Get It Published.* That's compared to six months for a response for unagented works. Agents get your book noticed, and they get personalized responses. This kind of attention can speed up the acquisitions process considerably.

There are many other pros and cons as well, as shown in the following list. You should know that agents:

Pros

Have established contacts within the industry

Know best practices for preparing a proposal

Are likely to get you a larger advance than you could get on your own

Can negotiate terms of the contract that you may not entirely understand (e.g., foreign rights, subsidiary rights, royalty structure)

Track your royalties and ensure you get paid

Act as your advocate if problems arise between you and the publishing house

Cons

Are another layer of gatekeeping

Can add six months to a year to the process

Take 15 to 20 percent of your advance

Beyond the cons listed here, fear of rejection seems to be one of the biggest holdups for aspiring authors. For whatever reason, it is less scary for many authors to skip the agent and go straight to the source. The decision is yours to make, but I have always felt, what is the harm in testing the waters? Your ultimate goal is getting your high-quality, highly marketable book in front of readers, and an agent may be able to help. Pinpoint the agents most likely to be interested in your work and see what happens. Maybe agents aren't interested in what you have to offer. But you might be surprised. If agents respond to you, you can decide from there whether you want to pursue the professional relationship. If no one responds, then you have more information about the amount of work you need to do to self-publish or to find another route. And while you are doing that, you can continue writing and polishing your manuscript.

I must note, however, that it is false to think that any agent is better than no agent. There are predatory agents out there. Protect yourself by educating yourself and working only with people you trust. You should not sign with someone who wants money up front, whether he or she calls it a reading fee, an evaluation fee, or any other name. Reputable agents do not get paid until they sell your manuscript. The article "How to Find a (Real!) Literary Agent" by the Science Fiction and Fantasy Writers of America advises that good agents will list recent book placements on their website; are accessible by means other than just e-mail; and won't try to sell you on other services. Membership in the Association of Authors' Representatives (AAR), the trade group for US literary agents, is also a plus. AAR has a searchable database that you can use to determine if your prospective agent is a member.

Whether you opt for an agent or not, if you are to be published by a traditional publishing house, you will work with an acquisitions editor.

WHAT YOU CAN EXPECT FROM YOUR ACQUISITIONS EDITOR

Some authors seem to think their acquisitions editor is their adversary, someone who has set out to destroy everything they loved about their manuscript. In truth, AEs are your advocate. After they have reviewed your proposal or sample chapters and decided this may be a project worth pursuing, they must then go before an editorial board and justify their reasoning. Just as you used a well-crafted marketing hook and knowledge of the competition to sell your book idea to your AE, he or she now has to sell it to the publisher, the marketing department, the sales department, the other acquisitions editors—all the people who make up the editorial board. AEs must demonstrate how this particular project is going to be worth the time and money it will take to produce it. And in so doing, they are putting

> **Inside Tip**
>
> The most important part of soliciting publishers and agents is to give them what they want. How do you know what they want? It might seem mysterious, but to a large extent they will tell you. Go to their website, look for "Manuscript Submissions" or a similar tab, and read everything they have to tell you about what to send, in what format, and how. Then do exactly what they want, to a T.

themselves on the line. They want you to succeed because it means they have succeeded.

So where is the rub? In working with an AE, you will quickly notice that you are not his or her only author. You are one of many, and you may have to wait your turn. Further, publishing houses often rank books in order of priority, so if your book is not an A-priority project, you may have to wait longer. That means that after you submit your manuscript, it may take one to two *months* for your editor to read the manuscript and make notations. Then, when you finally do receive the notations, you may be disappointed with how very much the editor wants to change. Where you may feel the hook for your book is one thing, the AE may see it as another and will try to steer you in that direction.

Why would this be? The acquisitions editor is more familiar with the market than you are and is doing his or her best to make sure your book is competitive with books already on the shelves. Try not to be offended. When you see the changes that your AE has suggested, remind yourself that you have opted to go with a publishing house in part because the editors there bring an expertise you don't have. If your entire vision for the book has been altered, you certainly have the right to argue your side, and in fact an author with no opinion can be as frustrating as one who holds too firm to his or her ideas. But you must be reasonable. Rather than arguing over every change (and I have seen this happen), pick your battles. This is your opportunity for a constructive back-and-forth discussion with someone who wants to help make your book truly marketable. Work together until you come to a consensus on the best path forward. If you have built up your own knowledge of the market and developed a strong marketing niche, as we will discuss in the Potholes at the end of this chapter, your conversations with the AE will be that much more productive.

At the other end of the spectrum, you may be dismayed to discover how little your AE has done to improve your work. To prevent this from happening, let your editor know that you are looking for and open to suggestions. "If you want your editor to go at your manuscript aggressively," advise Rabiner and Fortunato, "tell her that you want her to do whatever she thinks necessary to improve the manuscript." With open lines of communication, you are much more likely to get the kind of editing you want.

By contrast, some AEs won't attempt to shape the manuscript themselves and will instead send it to another editor, either someone in the development department of the publishing house or a freelance developmental editor (the subject of the next chapter). These AEs focus on acquiring—negotiating with agents and authors to bring a salable project into the company—and leave the nitty-gritty to those expert in "rearranging the furniture," as Scott Norton calls it in his book *Developmental Editing.* A vision will be set by you and the AE, but the real back-and-forth may come later.

As may be expected, given your AE's knowledge of the market, this key player on the publishing team will also be heavily involved in the marketing of your book. He or she will often write the cover copy and catalog copy (or at least initial drafts) and will prepare tip sheets for the marketing and publicity departments. Cover copy, for those unfamiliar with this term, is the marketing material you see on the back of your book. Hardcover books also have flap copy that appears on the book jacket; e-books may have abbreviated marketing copy or they may repeat the cover copy. Tip sheets list all the features of your book and the benefits your readers will get from those features. These sheets are used by the various people throughout the company who are involved in selling your book. Cover and catalog copy and tip sheets are key tools for the marketing and promotion of your book.

Selecting book titles and cover designs also come under the purview of acquisitions editors. When you submitted your manuscript, hopefully you spent a fair amount of time coming up with what you considered the best possible title. The AE and the editorial board may or may not agree with you, and titles often change more than once after acceptance. As author, you will be involved in these discussions but will not have the final say. Similarly, it is the rare book contract that gives the author final approval of the cover. The AE will ask for your input and will give you a chance to give your feedback, but you will not have final approval. To prepare yourself for this discussion, study the competition: look at the covers of similar books and see what everyone else is doing. Successful book covers are a lot like popular teens in high school: they fit in with the crowd but also manage to stand out with a fresh or new approach. So, educate yourself about what a good cover for your book might be by researching the competition. That way, if you really hate the cover that is suggested for your book, you will have a leg to stand on—you can point to the other books in your field to make your argument. See Chapter 5 for more on this topic.

WHAT YOUR ACQUISITIONS EDITOR EXPECTS FROM YOU

Perhaps what acquisitions editors expect most from their authors is that you remember they are human beings. This can be a challenge because they are often endowed with a romantic glow. However, like everyone else, they have limited time in their days and many projects to attend to. So be professional and courteous. Especially in the early phases, a call a month or a periodic e-mail can be the most effective way to make contact with your AE without damaging your relationship. A call a week, and especially a call a day, is more likely to anger your editor than to spur him or her to action.

Further, your AE expects you to trust him or her. Without trust in your editor—any kind of editor—the project will be a struggle every step of the way. If you are able to let go a little, your AE will be able to do his or her job much more effectively. It is helpful if you have an opinion about the direction your book should take and what the final product should look like, as opposed to being a blank slate, but flexibility is key.

Flexibility relates both to the content of your book and to your schedule in reviewing changes. Although it may not seem fair given how long you had to wait to hear back from your AE, you are expected to be readily available to discuss changes, and timeliness in returning revised manuscripts is only to your benefit. As Rabiner and Fortunato bluntly state, "Given the fact that you signed a contract . . . you'd be wise to keep your own calendar flexible, rather than boxing off dates."

You may also be expected to contribute to the marketing materials. Either your AE or the sales and marketing department will usually generate the cover copy for your book. You will then have a chance to review it, although, once again, you likely will not have final approval. Catalog copy is often handled the same way; however, some publishing companies will ask you to generate it yourself. This is one place where your knowledge of the market and the competition and your marketing hook are crucial.

The best authors for acquisitions editors tend to be those who are educated about the publishing process and who recognize that while publishing is a business, making a book together can be a truly enjoyable experience when all parties are doing what is expected of them.

ROADSIDE ASSISTANT

Denise Betts

Former acquisitions editor

Denise Betts spent several years as an acquisitions editor for NTC/ Contemporary Publishing Group, a division of McGraw-Hill that published nonfiction trade books in areas such as careers, business, and self-help. Here she shares her perspective on working with authors.

When you were an AE, what did you expect from your authors in regards to a good working relationship?
The best working relationships involve honesty and trust. I expect that my authors trust that I have their best interests at heart and that any comments, criticisms, or suggestions come from a place of goodwill and with the intention of improving the project. Authors need their editors to be honest with them about the expectations of the publishing house for the potential salability of the project, the intended market, and what design and positioning will be most beneficial to the project. Sometimes, however, honesty can

feel like an attack on something that's naturally very close to the author's heart. If the author can trust her editor, then together they can produce an even better book!

What were some of the common mistakes you saw?
One common mistake I often saw was authors having unrealistic expectations of the kinds of publicity, promotion, and marketing dollars the publishing house was going to put toward their book. Realistically, only a select few of the top books each season will get dollars allocated for publicity and promotion. Authors are often expected to have a platform of their own or do a fair amount of work getting the word out about their book. Another misconception was the amount of influence an author has over things like the marketing of their book or even the design of their book jacket. Contracts universally give the publishing house the final say in these matters, although authors may negotiate a consultation clause into their contract at signing.

What advice do you have for new authors?
Do your best to leave your ego at the door and not take things too personally. Your book wouldn't be under contract unless the publishing house thought that it was a good one. The process of realizing a book from idea to print involves a lot of individuals who all bring their opinions and expertise to the table, so be prepared for a highly collaborative process.

Can you share any best or worst author stories?
One of the best and worst involved a book that had two authors writing in two very different voices. It was a career/business book, and, unfortunately, both authors were not outstanding writers. In fact, one would write chapters that were essentially bulleted lists, and he couldn't understand how this was a problem. His coauthor, thankfully, did and was very open to letting me do a significant amount of writing, filling out his work. Eventually, the book was shaped into something that everyone was happy with, but it was a much more pleasurable experience working with the author who was open to hearing the criticisms of his work.

THE PROCESS

Either through your agent or as an individual, you will submit your book proposal to as many publishing houses as it takes to gain interest. After suffering through several rejections and nonresponses, you may find that you are the lucky recipient of "interest" in your book. From there you or your agent sets up a meeting with the acquisitions editor, either in person or over the phone, to discuss the project further. You are still trying to sell the book at this point. However, you should also use this time to assess the publisher to determine if this is the right match for you. (Recall Judy Lewin's experience from Chapter 1.) Listen closely to see what kinds of changes your editor wants to make, and determine if that vision for the book jibes with your own. The meeting may uncover that the book is not a good fit for the publishing house (or for you) and discussions end there; or the acquisitions editor may need to gather more details and then bring the book before the editorial board before making you an offer; or you may find yourself walking away from the meeting with a verbal offer on the table.

Inside Tip

Publishing is a small world. Be respectful of everyone you come in contact with. You might find that the editor you berated at one publishing house is now working at that new house you are trying to woo. If that's the case, your chances of acceptance have just been significantly diminished.

If the editor thinks your project is worth acquiring, he or she will next try to sell your book to the editorial board. In doing so, he or she takes your proposal or book query and adds some important material, including a profit and loss sheet, also called a P&L. These are the financials of the proposed project, an often optimistic painting of what the house stands to gain and how many units (books) would need to be sold in order to make a profit. Estimates of all expenses are included, as well as a suggested price point or price points. After much discussion, the board makes a decision. Hopefully for you that decision is to pursue the project.

From here it is negotiation time—when having an agent comes in particularly handy. You and the publishing house will discuss which rights you maintain and which you give up; what materials you will provide and what the publisher will take care of; an acceptable advance against the royalties and royalty rates; and other details of the relationship. Then you will agree to a specific date for turning in your completed manuscript. Do whatever you can to meet this deadline, and communicate with your AE if you are going to be late.

Once you have submitted your manuscript, your AE will read it and make notes, as described earlier in this chapter.

The next step is for you to respond to the editor's suggestions. You will be asked for an estimate on how long it will take for you to make these changes. Overestimate how much time you need, and then do your best to meet the deadline that you and the editor agree upon. During this period you may have some questions for your AE. Ask away, but it is always appreciated that if you call to discuss something, you are prepared with your questions and stay on topic. A common editor's quip is, "Do you want me to talk on the phone or edit your book?" Pleasantries are good, but be respectful of your editor's time. When you and the AE have come to an agreement about the final structure and content of the manuscript and all of these revisions have been made, you will move on to the production of your book, discussed in the following chapters.

– – – – – –

Your relationship with your acquisitions editor will continue throughout the production process, on to publication, and beyond. If you maintain a good relationship with your AE, you may find yourselves working together again on your next book endeavor.

AVOIDING THE POTHOLE
Improve Your Knowledge of the Market

Knowledge of the market refers to two complementary aspects of book publishing. One is a firm understanding of what the competition has to offer, and the other is using that information to develop a solid marketing hook. This knowledge is essential if you want to sell your book, whether that's to readers, agents, or acquisitions editors. Writing a book based on a solid understanding of the market also makes your AE's job easier as he or she sells your book to the editorial board and develops marketing materials for your book. Furthermore, by improving your knowledge of the market you will save money and time as you avoid the reworking of a manuscript that is often required when a writer has not done the necessary research.

Start by reviewing competing and comparable titles. What's the difference between competing and comparable books? The competition includes those titles directly competing for your readers, that is, books on the same topic, in the same genre, and with the same target market. Comparables may include books similar in presentation but on a different topic, or on the same topic but in a different format. This distinction is easy to see with books in a series: *Cover Letters for Dummies* is comparable to *Resumes for Dummies*, but it is not directly competing for readership. Comparables make good models for your own book and can bolster an argument for the acceptability of your idea in the market.

When you look at what other books are out there, you will discover what is standard

Inside Tip

If you are struggling with how to handle a specific writing challenge, want ideas about book cover designs, aren't sure whether you need to include subheadings in your table of contents, or have any number of other concerns, look at what the competition does. Don't be afraid to model your book after those that have been successful. Use the information available to you to craft the best, most competitive book you can.

for your genre or field and what is missing from the shelf, what the competition is doing and how you can do it better. Remember Scott Norton's advice: "A book's success also rests largely on whether it conforms to the market's expectations regarding length, tone, depth of coverage, and the inclusion of key features." If you are working with an AE, he or she will evaluate your manuscript on all of these points to determine how well it will stand up to the competition, and you should, too! Keeping these aspects in mind as you write will set your relationship with your AE on the right path and make your publishing experience smoother and more enjoyable.

But first things first. To analyze your competition, you have to find it. I recommend taking two paths: searching online and going to the bookstore.

RESEARCHING THE COMPETITION ONLINE

The most obvious place to start your online search for competitive books is the largest online bookstore, Amazon.com. Although Goodreads is fast becoming a major source of book information, Amazon (which owns Goodreads) is more comprehensive and simpler to navigate. The number of book titles listed on Amazon is estimated around 1.7 million; almost every book available, and even some that are no longer in print, can be found here. Amazon also offers some good sorting options. For instance, you can choose to sort by relevance, price, average customer review, or publication date. It is this last sorting option that I find most interesting for our purposes. For example, if you were interested in writing a book on New York Yankees shortstop Derek Jeter, a quick search for Derek Jeter books on Amazon pulls up 762 entries (up from 691 entries in January 2013). Roughly 8 of those books, each dedicated to the topic of Jeter, were published in 2012 alone, with another 5 published in the first half of 2013. You can also see what is due out soon; 5 more books either by or about Jeter were scheduled for 2014. That's a whole lot of competition for a book on Jeter. But finding competition shouldn't discourage you from writing your book; all of these titles also show that there is a huge market for baseball books, Yankees books, and, apparently, Jeter books. The key to success in such a market will be making yours stand out from the rest.

So does writing a book on Derek Jeter mean you're competing with 700-plus other titles? Not at all. First, not all of those entries are books. Second, not all of them will share your target market. To find the most relevant competition, start by searching for your working title. Make note of any other books with a similar or the same title that are also in the same genre. (That is, you probably don't have to write down nonfiction books on your topic if you're writing fiction.) Next, search for keywords related to your topic. Use a variety of keywords to surface as many potential competitors as you can. This will call up some unrelated titles, but look closely to find the ones that are similar. Read the synopses to determine if their target audience is the same as yours, and note the relevant books. Include the title, author, and synopsis for each in your notes. To find even more books, review Amazon's suggestive selling—the "Customers who bought this book also bought" list. Both comparable titles and more competition may be listed here. (Say what you will about this behemoth; it can't be denied that Amazon has nearly perfected the algorithm for suggestive selling.)

Several other websites are also helpful in finding your competition. Books in Print (www.booksinprint.com) from Bowker is a nearly exhaustive list, though it does require a subscription to access. Public and university libraries are also excellent resources.

Continue your search until you've found ten or so books that seem to target your audience and cover similar material as your proposed book. The section "Analyzing Competing Titles" later in this Pothole explains what to do with this information.

VISITING BRICK-AND-MORTAR STORES

If you can do all this research from the comfort of your home via the Internet, you may be wondering why you would drive to an actual

bookstore to find your competing titles. Although the sorting abilities on Amazon are great, there are many benefits to going to a store and reviewing the physical books you are competing with:

- ◆ You can see how big of a section your topic garners in a bookstore.

- ◆ You can see where in the store your section is located.

- ◆ You can evaluate books in your category that may not be on your topic but that illuminate your readers' other interests.

- ◆ You can determine the correct name for the category in which your book falls, important for being found by your target readership. (Is your competition shelved as true crime, history, or biography?)

- ◆ You can hold the competition in your hand, flip through the pages (all of them—not just those pages selected for the "Look Inside" feature online), and consider what you like and don't like.

If you can, locate the competing books you found online. Upon further inspection you may discover that one or more of the books you identified as competitors aren't targeting your readers after all. Or perhaps what sounded like a strong entry is actually very poorly written and won't be hard to outdo. Conversely, something you had nearly written off as a nonfactor may turn out to be your closest competitor, something for you to use as a benchmark.

Being able to look closely at each competing book gives you greater insight into what each actually has to offer. Angela Ruzicka, author of the successful children's book series Wendy on Wheels, reports reading countless children's books in researching her competition. "I spent three hours looking at every children's book in Borders. Then I went home and looked all over the Internet for positive books about children with different abilities. I found nothing like my vision." Angela found comparables but no direct competition. The series now includes four books and is read in English-speaking countries across the globe.

Next look for competing titles not previously uncovered on Amazon. Record the title and author for each of them, and add them to your list. If you have a smartphone you can easily snap a picture of the cover to record this information. If you don't have a camera on your phone, a pencil and paper will do the trick. Later you can find synopses and reviews for these books online. Again, this will be helpful when you begin the next step of analyzing these titles.

Finally, purchase the books you have deemed your nearest competition, either at the bookstore or via the Internet. Owning the books will give you the freedom to thoroughly inspect them (or even better, read them) and ensure that you are providing a superior product.

Fiction writers, even more so than nonfiction writers, should plan to read as much of the competition as possible. The selling points of fiction can be intricate and are not easily pulled out of the text just by skimming. Fortunately, most fiction writers already spend a fair amount of time reading the types of books they want to write. Still, performing thorough research of fiction is essential. You need to be sure that what you perceive to be a hole in the market is in fact a hole, and not just an area you have yet to discover.

What If There Is No Competition?

If you can't find any books that directly compete with yours, this may mean that you are on to something, but it also may be a red flag. Ask yourself, why has no one ever published in this area? Could it be that there isn't any interest in the topic, no market willing to buy the book? If you suspect the market just isn't there for your book idea, you may be able to resolve this problem by refocusing your book so that it fits into one of the markets that is already established. Your current focus may be too narrow, and if you were to expand your book in one direction or another, you could draw in a wider audience. This approach is worth serious consideration and should not be dismissed just because it means revising your manuscript.

If you have taken several years to write your book, you may need to do this exercise more than once to make certain you are fully aware of the realities of the market.

ANALYZING COMPETING TITLES

Take a look at the ten or so competing titles you have noted and narrow them down to the five or six that most directly compete with your proposed book. If all ten of the books you recorded are definitely hitting your topic and target market (as may be the case with the Derek Jeter books I uncovered), look more closely at the packaging of those books to see how your idea compares. Which books are about the same length as what you are planning? Which books are presented in the same format that you're considering, such as hardcover, paperback, or e-book? Do they contain the same supplementary materials you have planned? Are they targeting the same demographic? Do they strike the same tone you are aiming for? Consider all aspects to weed out the books that aren't actually competing with yours until you have a manageable list.

Next, take each competing title in turn and compare it with yours. Online research will reveal a wealth of information about the content of a book, but, as mentioned earlier, you can learn more specifics if you see the book in person. For an in-depth evaluation, read or skim the books you consider your closest competitors. (With fiction, skimming won't tell you what you need to know, so read away.) The point is to know exactly what the competition is offering so that you can make your book better than theirs. The following questions may help you with your analysis:

- ◆ How does the author's writing style compare to yours?

- ◆ Is the book an appropriate length for the target readers?

- ◆ Is the plot or argument fully explored and explained? Is it compelling?

- In nonfiction works and children's books, are there enough special elements such as boxes, charts, and illustrations to keep the reader interested?

- What is the quality of the artwork? Is there too much or too little?

- Are any appendixes, references, endnotes, or a glossary included?

- Is there an index?

- What kind of front matter—such as a preface, introduction, time line, list of illustrations, list of characters, or map—is provided?

- Does the book cover all of the essential information that readers are looking for?

- Does the story educate or entertain? Is it enjoyable?

As you answer these questions, consider what is included as well as what has been left out. Where does the competition succeed (what you should emulate) and where does it fall short (an opening for you to excel)? An analysis of competing books is a great way to find your niche. What will you provide that your competition doesn't? Further, the more you can build your knowledge of the market, the better you will be able to communicate with other publishing professionals and the better you will be able to sell your book.

ROADSIDE ASSISTANT

Bob Baker
Author and teacher

Bob Baker is an author, teacher, artist, and musician dedicated to showing creative people of all kinds how to get exposure, connect with fans, and increase their incomes. He is the author of *Guerrilla Music Marketing Handbook, 55 Ways to Promote & Sell Your Book on the Internet, Unleash the Artist Within,* and the upcoming *DIY Career Manifesto.* Bob's free e-zine, blog, podcast, video clips, and articles are available at www.fulltimeauthor.com, www.diycareer manifesto.com, and www.thebuzzfactor.com.

What research did you do for finding your niche? How did you spot the hole in the market?
It wasn't so much that I went out to find or discover a niche. It sort of found me. Since I was a kid I've had a deep interest in both music and the written word. That naturally led to me being a performing musician and a writer.

I've also always had an entrepreneurial instinct and was determined to find a way to make a living doing something I was genuinely interested in. In my mid-twenties I combined those two early passions (music and writing) for the first time and started publishing a local music magazine in St. Louis, Missouri. I ended up publishing it for ten years. During that decade I wrote columns filled with music marketing and career tips, organized music business panels and workshops, and had my first book published in 1993.

So my chosen niche was simply an extension of who I was. And I think that's the ultimate way to pursue a career as an author and/or make a living—find some aspect of yourself that fills a need or want in the marketplace. But the first important step in that process is not to look at the market but to look within and assess your talents, passions, and gifts.

What are the key benefits to having a marketing niche?
Marketing is a lot easier when you have a vision of who you are and what you offer, along with a clear idea of who your ideal reader and fan is. Especially if you're just starting out and have limited resources, you must make the best use of your time, money, and energy. Spraying a vague message to a general audience won't get you noticed, nor will it lead to connections with readers and sales.

Even if you have broad personal interests and writing styles, I suggest choosing one aspect of what you do to be your leading identity with the public. Make it very clear and focused. Also, come up with an ideal fan profile: Determine the gender, age range, and mind-set of the perfect reader who will be the most enthusiastic about your writing. Figure out where that type of person hangs out online and off. Go to those places and become part of the community. Communicate in a way that appeals directly to that ideal type of person.

What advice do you have for new authors who may be struggling with determining their niche?
Imagine a Venn diagram of three overlapping circles. One circle represents things you are passionate about or at least very interested in. Another circle includes talents and skills you have developed—things you are already very good at. The third circle represents a want or need in the marketplace that a segment of the population is willing to pay for.

Identifying only one or two of these circles could lead to trouble, such as losing interest in the subject or learning too late that few people are willing to spend money on what you have to offer. Think of everything you bring to the table related to your passions and skills. Make it a game to uncover some aspect of all that you are that you can "position" to attract an audience and generate sales.

Do you have any advice regarding marketing and/or making the most of your niche?
Once you have determined your niche, the best way to make an impact online is to create an abundance of "content" related to your topic or genre. And crank it out consistently over time.

That content can include blog posts, audio podcasts, YouTube videos, teleclasses, interviews, guest blogging, webinars, publishing short stories, giving away sample book chapters, and more. To keep your sanity, you don't have to do all of those things. Pick two or three that you enjoy creating and be relentless in producing and sharing free content in those preferred formats.

The more content you create on a specific topic, the more likely you will be discovered by people searching for that subject matter online!

AVOIDING THE POTHOLE
Develop Your Marketing Hook

After researching the other books on your topic and analyzing them to see how yours compares, you have likely determined where your book excels and where it is lacking. Use that knowledge to create a compelling hook and a winning sales handle. Acquisitions editors, agents, and readers are equally demanding of these important marketing features. For AEs and agents, a strong hook will help them sell your book to the next level up the chain of decision makers. Readers have many books to choose from; it's the sales handle and hook that will get them to choose yours.

THE HOOK

What makes your book worth publishing? Why would someone choose your book over a competitor's? The answers to these questions constitute your marketing hook. Agent-author Michael Larsen notes in his book *How to Write a Book Proposal* that your hook should be "the single most exciting thing . . . that makes your book sound new, needed, and timely." Presumably this is what got you excited about writing your book in the first place. If you've been working on your manuscript for a long time, however, or you know you have a lot of competition, you might not remember or recognize what is so special about your project. It's also possible that what you think is the hook is not really the most impressive, remarkable, and marketable element of your book idea. Try brainstorming with friends, family, and other writers to find out what they like about your idea. It may also help to step away from the project for a while and rejuvenate so that you can remember what made you want to write this particular book.

The following simple exercise will help you put into words exactly what your book has to offer. Think about the back cover of a book. Many times you will see a bulleted list with the heading "Inside You'll Find." If that were on the back of your book, what would it say? (Although this setup is most common for nonfiction books, it applies to fiction and poetry, too, so don't think you're off the hook if you're writing in one of the latter categories.) Try to come up with three to five bullet points that highlight what readers will get out of your book. If you're stumped, talk it over with a friend until you are able to distill the benefits of your book into single sentences or phrases. Here are some examples to get you thinking.

Nonfiction: *Derek Jeter: The Quiet Leader*

- More than 75 interviews with Derek Jeter's friends, family, and teammates

- An in-depth analysis of Jeter's highly regarded leadership style

- 10 key lessons from the field that improve relations and results in the boardroom

Fiction: *The Goblet of Calrimdor*

- A detailed, interactive fantasy world that invites the reader to make plot choices

- Strong, complex heroes and villains that capture the imagination

- Highly detailed maps and a glossary that bring Calrimdor to life

Poetry: *Walk with My Savior*

- 50 devotional poems about God and nature

- Original artwork by the author

- Space for journaling after each poem

> **Title Options**
>
> As you review the competition you may find yourself at a loss for a new and appealing title for your own book. In that case, I heartily recommend Scott Norton's book *Developmental Editing* for inspiration. The table Strategies for Creating a Working Title presents twenty easy-to-understand strategies for coming up with a title, along with their definitions and examples. I don't know about you, but until I read this helpful table I never would have guessed there were *twenty* ways to come up with a title.

Detailing the selling features of your book in this way will help you to (1) determine your hook and (2) see where your manuscript could be strengthened so that you are sure to get readers' attention. When you have identified your hook, you can use that to develop a more complete book package. With a complete book package, your reader is immersed in the world you have created from cover to cover. For example, a superior title reflects the content, tone, and hook of the book. Part and chapter titles relate to the book title. Any special elements also contribute to the overall tone of the book. *One Page at a Time: On a Writing Life* by Pat Carr is one good example of making full use of a marketing hook. This memoir is set up as one-page vignettes that flow together to tell the story of Carr's life as a writer. That's a fun and unusual way to present a memoir that may otherwise be lost in the crowd. If you are searching for an agent or traditional publisher, this type of complete package is often what they are looking for as they weigh whether to take on your manuscript and try to sell it.

THE SALES HANDLE

Have you heard of the thirty-second elevator pitch? The idea is that you need to be able to sell someone on your book idea in the amount of time it takes to ride an elevator from the lobby to the second floor. More recent research indicates that the time you have

to make the sale is closer to seven seconds. That means you have to be able to sum up your marketing hook in seven seconds, or about one sentence—what constitutes your sales handle. For the traditionally published author the sales handle (sometimes called a logline) will be used in a cover letter to catch the attention of agents and publishers. Self-publishers will use theirs on the back cover or in marketing materials.

Unless you are in advertising, or a poet, condensing a 65,000-word book into one sentence may seem impossible. It's not. It simply takes practice. Once again, looking at the competition can help.

Although not all books carry them, many back covers have a sales handle or tagline across the top that is intended to catch readers' attention. The more sales handles you read, the more you will notice a pattern or formula. They are often about ten words long, and they capture the tone of the book they are meant to sell. Like your hook, the sales handle should sum up why your book is worth reading. You will probably need to work through several iterations before coming up with a truly great sales handle. The following list offers real-life examples:

Nonfiction: Step into the garden with writer and rural historian Jerry Apps! (*Garden Wisdom* by Jerry Apps)

Academic: Quick, on-the-go access to essential medical-surgical nursing information! (*Clinical Companion for Medical-Surgical Nursing* by Kathy A. Hausman)

Adult Fiction: A political cataclysm strikes the United States (*Indivisible?: The Story of the Second American Civil War* by Paul Martin Midden)

Children's Fiction: Great little books for great little kids (Sandra Boynton board book series)

What is the common goal that most writers have when they publish a book? They want to share their thoughts and ideas with the world. To accomplish that, the book has to be appealing to readers. At the most basic level, a book's marketing hook is what makes it

desirable. The sales handle, then, is the fastest way to convey that hook to potential book buyers. A strong hook as well as a strong sales handle lead to more sales and, therefore, more readers benefitting from your work.

Mapping Out Your Road to Success

Research your competition to ensure that you are crafting the best, most marketable book.

Work only with agents and editors you trust.

Stay flexible when working with acquisitions editors, and take a collaborative approach to editing.

Develop your hook and use it to create a complete book package.

3

Looking at the Big Picture
Manuscript Development

Does your manuscript keep a consistent tone throughout? Does your manuscript address its audience appropriately? Is your book organized in the most effective way? Developmental editing is one of the best ways to get the answers to these questions. Not every manuscript will need development, but those that do won't get very far without it.

Developmental editors—also called DEs, substantive editors, or content editors—are often the first professionals to read your manuscript. They help to shape the overall structure and content of a book. You may work with one as part of the traditional publishing route, or you may hire one on a freelance basis to make sure your manuscript is in the best possible condition before you begin the publication process.

If not every manuscript needs development, how do you know if yours does? First, read this chapter to find out what a DE can do for you. Then, if you think you don't need one, get a second opinion. Contact a freelance editor and ask for an evaluation. The cost for an evaluation ranges from free to a few hundred dollars, depending on how in-depth of an assessment you want, but it's worth it. If the evaluation indicates your manuscript

> Manuscript development can be an uncomfortable process. You need flexibility, good communication skills, and a thick skin to thrive.

needs development, don't ignore this recommendation. If you skip development now, head into the next stages of book production, and two months later uncover a big-picture problem like an unclear audience, you may find it's too late in the game to fix it, or else you'll be spending incredible amounts of time and money reworking your manuscript.

The Potholes for this chapter, defining your audience and attending to permissions, both relate to areas that, if skipped, can require major rewrites if problems are discovered later. When you take the appropriate steps up front, you can save yourself significant time, money, and heartache.

When figuring your publishing schedule, allow two to six months for manuscript development. If you are hiring someone yourself, you can expect to pay between $45 and $75 an hour, depending on the genre and complexity of the book. If you are using a freelance DE arranged through your publishing house, you may be asked to cover the charges out of your advance. Some publishers, however, have in-house developmental editors whose services you would not have to pay for. In these cases the acquisitions editor is usually less involved in manuscript development and focuses on signing new projects, while the DE handles the editing.

WHAT YOU CAN EXPECT FROM YOUR DEVELOPMENTAL EDITOR

Developmental editors are concerned with the structure and content of your book. If your manuscript lacks focus, your DE will help you find the right direction to take (the "right" direction generally being the most marketable). This is where problems of inconsistent tone, an unclear audience, or an unidentified marketing niche often surface. Developmental editors perform many of the same editing tasks as an acquisitions editor, but unlike AEs, whose time is split between editing and the business side of publishing, DEs tend to be able to give you more personal attention. If you have hired a DE on a freelance basis, this is undoubtedly true. Either way, you will find that good DEs are friendly, organized, and creative, an uncommon mix that makes them extremely valuable to your endeavor.

Although these editors are mostly a friendly bunch, when working with a DE, be prepared to be challenged. Your DE, generally speaking, won't dictate to you what the book has to be, but you may be asked to justify your position when there is disagreement. At all times, however, it should be a collaboration. In his essay "Developmental Editing" Paul D. McCarthy writes, "Successful collaboration allows the author to feel sustained and liberated by knowing that she doesn't have to bear the burden of creation, development, and refinement alone." While it can be a relief to be able to lean on another's expertise, at the time of editing, this so-called liberation by your DE may feel more like an attack. It helps to remember that you and your editor have the same goal: making the best book possible. When you consider your DE a part of your publishing *team*, you will be better able to accept his or her criticisms.

When you work with a developmental editor, flexibility and good communication are a must. Manuscript development can be uncomfortable. The effort you have put into your writing, the time you took to craft the manuscript the best you could—it is difficult to set those aside and let someone else, an outsider, take apart and piece back together your work. To help smooth the process, discuss your vision of the book with your DE and work together until you can agree on a plan of action. Be open-minded and seriously consider the feedback that you are getting. It is essential that you and your DE have common goals and vision for the book for development to succeed. "If the author does not embrace the plan with enthusiasm," explains Scott Norton in his book *Developmental Editing*, "there's no sense in attempting development." Should you have real reservations about the direction the DE is leading you and you feel your vision for the project is in danger, talk to your AE, if applicable. If this is someone you have hired, you may wish to find a new DE. Following the guidance in the sidebar "5 Steps to Hiring a Freelance Editor" later in this chapter can help you avoid this problem.

Once you and the DE agree on the direction your book should take, you can move to the next level of detail. The DE will help you determine the best order and organization for the chapters, highlight places where the text may have digressed too far from the topic, and point out areas where more explanation is needed. If you are writing nonfiction, the chapter titles, headings, and subheads in the book may need to be rejuvenated, reworked, or eliminated. Artwork, sidebars, and any other special elements may also need to be created or placed throughout the manuscript. With fiction, common errors that DEs deal with include points of plot that don't lead anywhere, inconsistent characterization, or missed opportunities to bring out your main themes. Throughout the process the DE will help ensure that your intended audience is clear and that you have maintained an even tone in your writing.

Who Needs Beta Readers?

If you have spent any time in the writing community in the past five to ten years, you have probably heard about beta readers. These are colleagues, acquaintances, and other writers who read your manuscript for free and give you feedback. They do not replace editors, but they are a very helpful addition to the manuscript development stage. It's possible that with good beta readers you could avoid the cost of a DE and head straight to copyediting.

The value of beta readers depends largely on whom you enlist for help. A good reader has some interest in your topic or genre, is an enthusiastic reader, and is not afraid to tell you the truth about your writing. Often, friends and family are not the best beta readers because they do not want to hurt your feelings. You need people who have enough distance from you that they feel free to tell you the hard truths. I recommend looking for a variety of people to help you—for example, readers who represent your target audience, those with very strong writing skills of their own, as well as someone who is coming to the book with no prior background in the subject. What you do with the feedback you get from your beta readers is up to you. I suggest neither fighting every criticism nor acquiescing to every change. Evaluate each recommendation and determine if it helps you to reach your goals for the book.

In manuscript development you are piecing together the big picture rather than focusing on grammar, word choice, and punctuation. Those smaller types of corrections will be made later in the process.

WHAT YOUR DEVELOPMENTAL EDITOR EXPECTS FROM YOU

Most DEs will expect a certain level of trust and respect from you. They have an advantage that allows them to improve your manuscript in a way that you can't on your own, and much of this comes from not being emotionally tied to the writing, as you are. They will put in many hours of work on your project, but when they see your manuscript for the first time, they can spot the rough areas much more easily than you can. And because they have been doing this kind of work for a long time, they also will be able to provide some relatively easy solutions to those problems. In the case of your publishing house requiring you to work with a DE when you didn't think one was necessary, you will also have to put your trust in the acquisitions editor who set you on this path.

In addition to trust, timeliness is another trait DEs appreciate. Your DE will work hard to meet the agreed-on deadline for sending you the edited manuscript, and you should work similarly hard to return the reviewed manuscript by the due date you have agreed to. Meeting this deadline is important because your DE has other authors to accommodate as well. If you miss your deadline, your DE may need to put your book at the back of the pile when you do return the manuscript. For some authors, scheduling is flexible, but if you are trying to meet a certain publication date and you miss your deadlines, you cannot expect your DE to make up the time. So be realistic about your ability to finish the manuscript review, and communicate with your editor if you need more time.

When the DE and the author are able to agree on a vision for a new project, development can be a thrilling experience. For me as a DE, I love seeing a manuscript transform from one with gaps and excesses into something whole and compelling. Helping an author to achieve the vision he or she had for the book is extremely rewarding. When there is a struggle at every turn, however, the quality of the end product is in doubt and the project loses its luster. But with a talented and engaged author, my suggestions are assessed, adapted, and implemented in the author's own voice and style, and the final manuscript is a point of pride for both of us.

ROADSIDE ASSISTANT

Kristina Blank Makansi
Developmental editor

Kristina Blank Makansi is cofounder of Blank Slate Press, an award-winning small press in St. Louis, Missouri, and a partner in Treehouse Publishing Group, an author services company also located in St. Louis. She has edited both fiction and nonfiction and is also an author. Her historical fiction work, *Oracles of Delphi*, is in revisions, and she has written and is self-publishing *The Sowing*, the first in a New Adult science-fiction trilogy, cowritten with her two daughters.

As a DE, what do you expect from your authors in regards to a good working relationship?
A good working relationship can only exist if both editor and author are good listeners—even if the "listening" is done through e-mail. The author must be willing to listen and to refrain from the reflexive "yes, but . . . " comeback when challenged. The first thing I want to know is what the author is trying to accomplish with the particular work. I want to read the synopsis, the query/pitch, and the logline so I know up front what the author believes the story is about and what she has (or hopes she has) accomplished. I may be just one reader, but if something isn't working for me, then there is a good chance the author hasn't achieved her goal for the work. A good working relationship will allow me to be frank and to point out how and why I think the story doesn't work, without

the author taking it personally or dismissing the criticism because she is in love with the passage/concept/plot point, and so on.

A professional author must understand that suggested edits and pointed critiques are not personal attacks, and a professional editor must always strive to be helpful and to offer constructive feedback without being dismissive or rude.

What are some of the common mistakes you have seen?
It may be cliché to cite the "show, don't tell" issue, but it is a common problem. Another is too much backstory too soon—before the reader has had a chance to care about the characters in the first place. Many authors also fall back on dialogue to explain backstory or to tell the reader something that could be more powerfully shown a different way, say through a character's action or even what the character doesn't say. Also, a very common mistake is to think that describing what someone looks like tells the reader anything at all about who the person is. Physical description is helpful, but a story moves forward and a reader keeps turning the pages because of the characters' motivations, not their age or hair color. Finally, authors all too often fall back on what's easy—starting a book or chapter with a description of the weather, for instance. One writer I respect said once that if he read a chapter that started with a description of clouds, he damn well wanted those clouds to pick up the gun on the mantle and shoot the main character before the end of chapter one.

What advice do you have for new authors?
Read. Read. And did I mention read? It is critical for authors not only to read books and short stories that are critically acclaimed but also to read works from other authors who write in their genre and who are at a similar stage in their professional publishing career.

I also recommend authors get to know other authors by attending, if possible, workshops and conferences or by connecting online. It's a great idea to join a book club to discuss books with other readers (people who are not writers) as well as to join a writing group.

What differences do you see between in-house and freelance development, in particular regarding the author's experience of it?
As publisher and editor of a small press and as an editor for an author services practice, I've edited both as an in-house editor and as a freelance editor. As a traditional in-house editor, I have a lot more say over the final manuscript. While I would never dream of being dictatorial over some changes, an in-house editor can choose to not go forward with a project if the author refuses to make certain changes to a manuscript. An in-house editor will take on a project not only because they have fallen in love with it but also because they have a particular vision for it. If the author refuses to make the changes necessary for the work to fit the editor's vision, then the project may very well end up dead in the water. While this may not happen very often, the publishing house and the editor have final say over the manuscript (and the title and the cover . . .).

In contrast, the freelance developmental editor's role is to help the author write the best manuscript the author can possibly write without imposing the editor's vision on it. As a freelance editor, I may *strongly advise* an author to make a particular change, but the author is free to ignore me. The author is the one with ultimate control of the project, and my job is to help him or her make the best editorial decisions possible within the framework of the goals for the project.

THE PROCESS

The difference in the developmental editing process between traditional publishing and self-publishing is largely a matter of who is doing the hiring. It's possible that you could use a freelance DE before approaching a publishing house or that your publisher suggests you work with (and pay for) one before it accepts the manuscript. In those cases, your process will be more aligned with the self-publisher's. However, self-publishers have as much time in their schedules as they choose. Traditionally published authors need to adhere to the schedules of their publishers. If you write fiction, plan to have the development done before you approach a publisher; fiction is rarely developed after it has been acquired.

Traditional Publishing

As with most editor-author relationships, you may never meet your developmental editor in person. Instead, your communications will be via e-mail and the phone.

The process begins when your acquisitions editor hands the manuscript over to the developmental editor. You will most likely receive an e-mail from your DE introducing herself and setting out some scheduling information. Not much is required of you at this time except perhaps to approve the proposed schedule and set aside time to review the editing.

To start, your DE will read the entire manuscript, take notes, and then discuss with you the direction she thinks the book should take. Some major problems may be uncovered, such as an unclear audience or inconsistent tone, or it might be more a matter of spicing up the headings, reorganizing the chapters, and smoothing transitions. Either way, your DE will have suggestions and a vision for the book, and the two of you will need to come to a consensus on how to proceed.

After this initial discussion, your DE may return the manuscript and have you make the agreed-on changes based on her extensive notes and suggestions. This is particularly true if there is significant rewriting to be done, in which case your editor may offer guidance but leave it to you to figure out the details. In other instances, the DE will do most of the work herself before returning the manuscript via e-mail. What she can't fix, she will query for you to tackle. She will give you a deadline and ask you to confirm your availability. Be up front about whether or not you can meet this deadline. There is usually some leeway, but your DE will be planning her schedule around you, so rather than being optimistic, be realistic—and then meet your deadline.

As you work through the DE's changes and suggestions, try to address each query as fully as possible. If you don't like a suggested change, rather than simply reverting to what you had before, consider if there might be a third option that satisfies both of your concerns. Go through the manuscript carefully, and compile any questions for your DE so that you can address them systematically over the phone. You may find you go through this routine a few times—the editor makes suggestions, you make changes, the editor reviews those changes and suggests others, and so on. If the schedule is tight or the manuscript very long, you may be asked to return the manuscript a few chapters at a time so that the next step in the process, copyediting, can begin even while you iron out the kinks in later chapters.

It's important to note that different editors have different styles. If you are open to having your whole book taken apart and put back together, let your DE know that. If she gets the impression that you will fight every change, she may hold back, and then you are less likely to get the best possible product. That said, if your vision for the book is being significantly altered, speak up. The best editing is a collaborative approach in which the editor supports and guides you to improve the manuscript while maintaining your voice and achieving your agreed-on vision.

Inside Tip

Editing today is done electronically using the Track Changes function in Microsoft Word. If you aren't familiar with it already, get familiar with it now. It is extremely useful, but it can be overwhelming if you have never used it before, and you don't want to spend precious time learning a new program function when you should be revising your manuscript.

Self-Publishing

Self-publishers looking for help developing their manuscript are tasked with hiring a developmental editor themselves (see the sidebar "5 Steps to Hiring a Freelance Editor"). Some authors seeking a traditional publisher will also hire a freelance DE to help them get their manuscript in shape before approaching agents and publishers. If you write fiction, this is probably you. The specific tasks of the freelance DE versus an in-house DE are largely the same, but the responsibilities of the author change.

The two biggest differences are that the author has more control over the schedule and more control over the changes that are made. Whereas an in-house DE has the backing of the publisher for his vision for your book, in this case you are the publisher. Therefore, you have the final say on the direction your book takes. Your DE is there to give his opinion; what you do with it is up to you. If you have a good relationship, your DE will feel comfortable pushing back when there are issues he feels you are not considering fully. If you run roughshod over him, though, you will get the book you want, but it might not be the best or most marketable book possible. That responsibility of knowing whether yours or your DE's opinion is the right one is what makes self-publishing so challenging and so rewarding.

The process for developing nonfiction is covered in detail in the previous section, "Traditional Publishing," but the process for developing fiction is somewhat different. For one thing, fiction works are more likely to be developed in one shot rather than with the back and forth that is common with nonfiction. For another, the editor is less likely to do substantial rewriting and will instead ask pointed questions and offer guidance on revisions for you to execute. Although some freelance DEs may work with both fiction and nonfiction, for the best developmental editing of fiction, you may opt for an editor with a master of fine arts degree (MFA). These editors tend to have more experience with fiction than those without an MFA. This is particularly important for those writing literary fiction, where knowledge of literary theory may be helpful.

No matter the genre, developmental editing is a difficult task. For that reason, you will pay more for this service than for copyediting. Consider it a question of value added. Much of the DE's time is spent conceptualizing and mulling over problems to find the best solution for your book. These skills are hard to come by and can make the difference between a book that sells and one that stalls.

5 Steps to Hiring a Freelance Editor

No matter what kind of editor you are hiring—developmental editor, copyeditor, or proofreader—the steps to finding the right one for you are virtually the same. A bad editor can do more harm than no editor, so do your homework before you hire someone.

1. **Gather the names of editors who work on books in your field or genre.** If you know other writers who have worked with an editor, ask them for a referral. If you can't find someone through word of mouth, check the Internet for databases; the Editorial Freelancers Association (www.the-efa.org), for example, has an expansive listing of various kinds of editors and other publishing professionals for hire. Also available to you are online sites such as oDesk.com, eLance.com, and others. These are good sources for finding lots of editors, but be sure to vet your editor before hiring. Because of the nature of these sites, where editors are bidding on your project to ensure you the lowest price possible, you are not assured of the highest quality.

2. **Research your potential editor.** If the editor has a website, read it. Look for testimonials, client lists, and any other information that will tell you if this is the kind of person you want to work with. Be sure you are hiring a *book* editor with substantial experience in *book* editing, and not just an English major passing himself or herself off as an editor. What's the difference between an English major and an editor? Editors have been trained through an editing class or certificate program or through on-the-job experience in an editing position, and they know how to use the pertinent style guides and other tools of the industry. Unfortunately, there are a lot of frauds out there, so be thorough in your research.

3. **Call or send an e-mail to your potential editor.** Tell the editor the working title of your book, briefly what it's about, the genre, the word count, and a little bit about yourself. If you have a deadline in mind, include that now. Also mention if you are planning to self-publish or find a traditional publisher (if you know). An editor is not an agent, so you do not need to include marketing information or a proposal unless requested. If your editor has met your criteria so far and seems open to your project, go to step 4.

4. **Ask for a quote, sample edit, and scheduling information.** A sample edit is five to ten pages from your manuscript that the editor marks up for free or for a nominal fee. This allows the editor to determine what level of editing you need—you may be in the market for copyediting, for example, but the editor thinks development is in order—and how long it will take. The sample edit allows you, the author, to see what kind of changes your manuscript is likely to receive. Use this to determine if you like the editor's style and whether it fits what you are looking for.

   Note that a sample edit is not the same as a manuscript evaluation. A sample edit should be cheap or free; the editor is trying to get your business. Manuscript evaluations, which are much more in depth and involve reading and assessing your full manuscript, tend to run a few hundred dollars.

5. **Evaluate what you have learned and add the crucial element of personality.** When determining if this editor is *the one*, consider qualifications and scheduling as well as personal compatibility. Are you comfortable with this editor's qualifications? Did you like the changes you saw in the sample edit? Do you trust this person to give you the best edit possible? Do you communicate well? Editing can be emotionally challenging for writers. It helps if you have an editor who matches your personality.

- - - - - -

How do you know when manuscript development is complete? When your book has a firm beginning, middle, and end, with chapters in their appropriate places and chapter titles and headings (if any) appropriate for the topic and genre. When the manuscript has a consistent voice and a clear focus. When you know what you are trying to accomplish with your book, and this manuscript achieves those goals. When you have all these things in place you are ready for the next step in the process: copyediting!

AVOIDING THE POTHOLE
Define Your Audience

"My book is for everyone. I want everyone to read it." Many a novice writer has responded this way when asked who the audience is for his or her book. Although that tactic may seem to offer the greatest appeal to agents and the widest possibility for sales, the truth is, your book is not for everyone. If you have written it that way, then you have some rewriting to do. Problems with audience manifest themselves as an uneven tone or a split focus in the book. Often, the book is trying to do too many things and, therefore, does none of them well. This is a common problem that arises during manuscript development, but it can be resolved early with the right planning on your part.

ANALYZING YOUR TARGET AUDIENCE

"You can't just think about what you're selling; you must also think about what your potential readers are buying." Michael Larsen, author of the bestselling book *How to Write a Book Proposal*, gives that advice when talking about how to create a great sales handle for your book. It's excellent advice for making your book sound appealing to your potential readers, but to follow it you have to know who those potential readers are. A wide range of elements factor into how you define your target market, and they can be broken down into three main categories: the demographics of your readers; their sophistication as readers, which directly relates to the tone of your book; and the region in which you are selling. To assess these factors, you may have to do a little research into who makes up your audience. Investigating your audience can be a lot of fun, however, as it largely involves getting out there and mingling with the people who share your interests.

Demographics: What Do Your Readers Look Like?

It sometimes seems crude to speak of people based on their demographics. Most of us like to think that we don't see race, age, ethnicity, or any other divisions. We are all humans, right? Unfortunately, when you are trying to reach an audience, it's not that simple. Rather than the melting pot analogy, human beings tend toward the birds of a feather analogy. And those birds of a feather tend to read the same books. So, when you describe the audience or market for your book, think about which groups—which demographics—you are writing for.

For those writers who have never considered this before, it may help to visualize the audience you would read your book to. If your book is for children, what age range do they fall into? How do they interact with the book? Is there a particular ethnicity or culture that you are trying to reach? If you are writing adult nonfiction, are your readers academics or average Joes? Are they older or younger, conservative or ready to dive into something new? Consider not only who will read your book but also who will buy it. Gift books, self-help books, and children's books may all be purchased by people other than your intended reader. You will need to balance this divide in your writing as well as your marketing.

Next, go to where your audience is. If you belong to an association based around your topic, take a look at the membership of that organization to determine who makes up your audience. These organizations are innumerable, covering nearly every topic and genre, from the Romance Writers of America to the American Association for Clinical Chemistry. If you don't belong to any such organization, consider joining one now. This is a great and fun way to get in touch with your target market and increase your marketing outlets. (Notice how the same elements that make your book stronger also make your author platform stronger? This is often the case.)

Think about the organization membership critically. What is the age range? What is the race makeup? What is the prevailing gender? What is the education level? Do the members seem to have other likes and dislikes in common? Expand your research beyond physical meetings; virtual meet-ups and social media sites such as Facebook, Twitter, and Pinterest can tell you even more about the people who read books on your topic. Also go to the bookstore or library and watch the people who browse your area. As you look around at your potential readers, use your eyes and ears, and be ready to adjust your preconceived notions.

If you're still having trouble outlining the demographics of your audience, the contrast of the next two examples might help. First, a biography of Derek Jeter. Who is going to be reading this book? As a Jeter enthusiast, you may think that everyone can learn something from Jeter's story. However, you have to decide whom you most want to reach with this particular book. Let's start with what age group you have in mind. If you are writing for ten-year-olds, the audience will be heavily tilted toward boys. If you're looking at an older audience, you have to consider that it's still sports, so more men than women will be interested, but you can't rule out women entirely. Women in general love memoirs, and the handsome Jeter has a special appeal. (This is made obvious by the fact that Pinterest has a whole search category for "shirtless Derek Jeter" items.) Other descriptors of your audience may include sports enthusiasts, particularly baseball fans; biography lovers; perhaps more African Americans than other baseball books might draw, as Jeter's father is African American; New Yorkers; and, of course, Yankees fans around the country. Note that defining your audience in this manner will not prevent the sixty-five-year-old Asian female hardcore baseball fanatic from buying your book, but she will not be the focus of your marketing campaign and will not directly affect how you write your book.

Now compare that audience analysis to that for a flaxseed cookbook. Who is the audience of this book? Cooks come in all shapes and sizes, but with a focus on flaxseed, this book will have a narrower audience than a general cookbook might have. Flaxseed is considered a health food, which tends to attract twenty-five- to sixty-five-year-old men and women interested in health and fitness, as well as other "foodies." Healthy eating trends can also be regional, with the coasts being more trendy than the middle of the country. But don't let those assumptions be the end of your audience description. Attend cooking classes, shop at the "foodie" stores, and watch the people in bookstores who buy these kinds of cookbooks so that you can accurately define exactly whom your book is for. When you look closely, you may be surprised by the people you find.

An important consideration here is whether you are uncovering people of a demographic who have not been reached by what is currently on the market. If you have noticed that a lot of fifteen-year-old girls are interested in baseball novels, yet you can't find any books that fit that model, that may be a niche to be explored.

For those working with a developmental editor, he or she won't go to the bookstore with you but will be able to tell if you haven't done your homework. For example, a good DE will point out when your flaxseed cookbook manuscript switches focus from, say, a beginning cook to an experienced chef. Identifying the demographics of your audience and writing specifically for those people will make development go more smoothly and will ultimately save you time and money in the editing process.

Region: Where in the World Does Your Audience Live?

How broad, geographically speaking, is the appeal of your topic? You may, once again, be tempted to say your book is for everyone, everywhere. For most new authors, however, that isn't true. So, be honest. Is the market for your book worldwide? In North America? The United States? The West? Nebraska? Omaha? A neighborhood in Omaha?

Being able to nail down the geographic location of your audience is important for two reasons. First, it can help you determine the breadth of your topic. For instance, if you are writing a book about Nebraska law and you know the law only in Nebraska, you don't want to get distracted by Iowa law or Kansas law. Focus on your expertise. With this niche you can pinpoint your marketing to get the most return on your investment. Conversely, if you are writing about Native Americans in Nebraska, you may see that your topic overlaps with stories about other Native American tribes and that you could easily broaden your appeal to the surrounding states and even the West as a whole by including those other stories. Suddenly you have grown your audience fivefold and have many more outlets for marketing and sales. This could be a real boon. A word of caution, however: If you find your regional appeal is small, be careful not to manipulate your book into something bigger than you are capable of doing well simply to gain a larger audience. A good, targeted book has more value than a mediocre, wide-ranging book.

The second reason it's important to evaluate your regional appeal is that it can help you focus on the agents, publishers, and marketing outlets interested in your book. Every publisher and agent has areas of interest. When you know what region your audience lives in, you can research and approach those publishers and agents who deal specifically with that kind of book. You can also target specific bookstores, associations, museums, or other venues either to carry your book or to host a book signing or book talk. This way you are not wasting time on people and places that are not interested in your project.

To determine the geographic area for your audience, start with the part of the world where you live and where the story—whether fiction or nonfiction—takes place. Then move outward. Stop when you reach your best estimate of who will want to buy your book. If your book has a naturally small audience, embrace it. Remember, niche is good. As you do your research, you may find that your book is of interest nationwide, yet you may have a better return on investment with a narrower approach. Particularly if you're self-publishing, a smaller niche may work to your advantage.

Tone: What Level of Sophistication Do Your Readers Have?

So, you know a little more about the demographics of your audience and where they live. Now you have to combine that with the tone you want to strike with your book. This factor has big implications for your writing style and how you will position your book

in the market. Age and education level of your intended readers will be the biggest drivers of what the right tone is.

Before we go any further, let's define *tone*. I use this term to describe the general attitude of your book. Is your writing friendly, technical, accessible, academic, confrontational, or humorous? Are you looking to pick a fight, teach a lesson, entertain, or engage your audience in a conversation? These questions are important because you will adjust your word choice, sentence structure, and even the title and the cover of your book to reflect the tone you choose. You may also approach different agents, publishers, or bookstores based on the sophistication of your writing and that of your audience. Furthermore, identifying the right tone for your audience ensures that you aren't marketing to laypeople a book full of technical or academic jargon, or a book full of slang to speakers of English as a second language.

Look again at our book on Derek Jeter. If we have set our audience at ten-year-olds, the tone of writing in this book will be less technical and more accessible, with shorter sentences and simpler terminology, than it would be for adult readers. It will have a lot of photos and sidebars to engage the younger reader and enliven the text, and it may have a variety of statistics at the back for diehard young fans. Conversely, if the book is for adults, we may choose a more complex tone: technical descriptions of Jeter's play, a confrontational look at his relationships outside of baseball, or an in-depth analysis of how he fits into the grand scheme of Yankees history. These writing-style decisions are based on the information you want to convey and what you know about your audience's sophistication as readers. By spending time with your target audience and reading other books aimed at your audience, you will discover what is and is not an appropriate tone for your book.

Do not underestimate the importance of determining the right tone. I have worked with several authors who struggled with their decision about how technical, how academic, or how casual their tone should be. Knowing your target audience and gearing your book's tone to appeal to that audience is something you need to do early on. Readers can tell when you have not quite settled on

a tone, and your book will suffer because of it. Revising for tone is doable, but the sooner you know the age and education level of your intended audience, the better you will do at keeping an even tone throughout your book. This is just one more area where you can save time and money in the editing process and give yourself an edge by planning your book ahead of writing it.

DETERMINING THE AUDIENCE FOR A CHILDREN'S BOOK

In all my conversations with authors about audience, the ones who seem to have the most trouble are children's book authors. The problem most often is a matter of too wide an age range. Ages nine to twelve may be a reasonable grouping, as these kids have similar reading ability and relate to characters in a similar way. Ages zero to six, however, encompasses so many stages of development that it may not be possible for an author to write appropriately for all children in this demographic. Beyond just the writing style, book formats range dramatically for this age group. Consider that children up to age two are prone to putting books in their mouths. Before age three, traditional paper pages will be ripped out. That's why there are so many cardboard and soft plastic books for children ages zero to three years. Books for older children may also be read to the zero- to three-year-old group, but those kids are a secondary audience. To pinpoint your primary audience and to fine-tune your vision for your book, consider the following questions:

- ◆ How many words will be on each page?
- ◆ How many pages will the book be?
- ◆ What material should the pages be made out of?
- ◆ Is there a narrative or are the children learning new vocabulary?
- ◆ Are there even words at all?

You must analyze in very practical terms how your book is going to be used so that you know (1) what to include in it, (2) what format it will take, and (3) how you are going to sell it to agents, children, and parents. With this information you will also be able to locate the competition more easily, an extremely important step in formulating your business plan.

Another challenge children's book authors face is that parents as well as youngsters have to like the book. Bright colors and a pony might be enough to catch the eye of the child, but the purchaser may want more. That's why if your children's book is narrative in form, I recommend including a lesson or a moral. Doing so will make it more appealing to adults—the people who actually buy the book—and what's more, if you have the ear of a young person, why pass up that opportunity? Be a positive influence.

ROADSIDE ASSISTANT
Tim Hill
Author and speaker

Tim Hill is the author of the Joe the Crab children's book series and an accomplished speaker. His books include *Joe the Crab Takes a Walk*, *Joe the Crab Hunts for Shells*, and *Joe the Crab Goes for a Swim*.

What was the hardest part about defining your audience?
For me it was gauging not where my age group began but where it ended. It took a while, but I've deduced that my books top out for *most* children around age nine. Learning who the actual buyers of books for the target kids were and how and when to target them was difficult, too. The timing part is still difficult and is a work in progress for me.

What did you do to help you solve these problems?
One of the ways I figured this out was not solely by sales (though clearly that helps) but through the speaking events I've been

doing for a while now. After a few events, I could just see it and sense it. I could even figure it out by taking into account which grade semester they were in; by the early months of the fourth grade you can see a new stage of maturity in their reading begin to form and how they look at you differently. So the third grade was the beginning of the last span of their development that had a big enthusiasm for "Joe."

Regarding the buyers, the obvious part is [targeting] moms, aunts, and grandmas. The not-so-obvious part is how to find them and when to target them. I found a bunch on Twitter, some on Facebook, and others through doing the "boutique" charity events. The holiday season is the best time to sell children's books, and having a book signing/release party event is a great way to gain some attention. The speaking events at schools are where a lot of kids and therefore parents and teachers learn about me. Social media is key, and it's hard to learn how to make it effective. But that's where the target groups are to connect with.

What advice do you have for new authors?

1. Take your time. Do it right, especially if it's your first publication. Mind your reputation from the get-go.

2. Research and plan when you're going to release your book and ensure that you get as much attention on it as possible, including planning an event to do so. Don't let your newbie status deter you—make that work for you. It's cool being a "new author," actually.

You'll have to get over yourself if you don't like the spotlight on you for that singular book release event. If you want folks to know about your book, you've got to be at least a temporary extrovert. I know that's not easy for authors, even counterintuitive for most of them. But stepping out for just a couple of hours could be very rewarding and even surprising to realize how much you know about your subject. At the same time, don't be shocked if you sell only a couple of books at your first release party/book signing. (By

the way, don't call it a book signing. People *get* to go to a "release party" because of the air of exclusivity. You *have* to go to a book signing.)

What are your thoughts on dealing with rejection?
It became clear fairly quickly that some of my adult writing friends didn't like my first children's book. They were very happy for me and sincere, but let's just say it was obvious they weren't genuinely impressed *enough* with my first offering. I'm one of those who would rather be told a brutal truth than be told something's great when it isn't and wonder. So I wish I'd had a little more opinion thrown my way—I figured it out anyway.

Nevertheless, rejection isn't fun. But, I experienced two things: (1) I quickly picked up suggestions and figured out ways to improve my first book, and (2) my target audience responded with almost nothing but positive feedback. The kids were diggin' it, and that's all that mattered to me. So an overhaul wasn't necessary.

Now, I have shored up that first book in various ways (and also the subsequent two): a little bit with the writing, some with the illustrations, some with the fonts, the author page, and other items here and there. So the journey's turned out pretty well over a couple of years now.

I'm now considering a hardback.

Your target audience will directly affect not only how you craft your book but also how you market it. A developmental editor can be influential in achieving the tone and focus that your book needs to resonate with your readers. To define your audience well, you must get involved in the appropriate communities and have a discerning eye. When you look around at the other people interested in your topic, what do you see? Look critically and you will be able to both visualize and describe your target market. When you can do that, you can ensure that your manuscript is hitting the right note, from cover to cover.

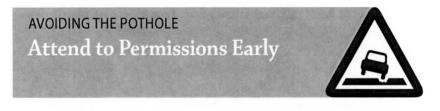

AVOIDING THE POTHOLE
Attend to Permissions Early

Throughout manuscript development, you may be continuing your research to fill in any holes that the developmental editor or your beta readers have uncovered for you. As you do this, you will probably come across certain passages in other works that you want to excerpt. Do you need permission? That depends on a number of factors. Lucky for you there are guidelines and resources that you can use to help navigate this ocean of uncertainty. If you are working with a DE, he or she will be able to guide you as to which passages require permission; however, taking the lead in requesting permission as soon as you know you want to use an excerpt can save you several months of waiting.

Some of the more commonly accepted rules regarding copyright infringement concern the length of the excerpt, the importance of the excerpt to the whole of the original work, and the type of work you are preparing. Items that generally require permission include long excerpts of prose and *any* quotes from poetry or music. That's right—if you plan to have epigraphs or other excerpts from music or poetry, plan to seek permission, no matter the length.

The definition of a long excerpt of prose is up to interpretation and is mitigated by the other two factors: importance of the excerpt to the whole of the original work and the type of work you are preparing. Many people, including some of the major traditional publishers, consider any prose excerpt less than a hundred words fair use (i.e., not requiring permission). This assumes that the work you are quoting from is substantially longer than a hundred words. That guideline won't keep you from being sued, but it is a helpful benchmark. As to the type of work you are preparing, you may not need to obtain permission if you are using the excerpts as part of your analysis in an academic book. Most other works are held to the standards just mentioned.

Besides fair use, there is another time when you might not need permission. These are excerpts from works that fall into the so-called public domain. This means that the material is no longer protected under the laws of copyright and does not require permission. How do you know if your excerpt is from a work in the public domain? Briefly, works published before January 1, 1923, are now in the public domain. Works published after 1978 are protected for at least ninety-five years, possibly longer if the copyright has been renewed. And finally, works published between 1923 and 1978 may or may not be in the public domain; you will need to search the records of the Copyright Office to be certain. For that, you are encouraged to use a copyright attorney or a search firm. (Permissionsgroup.com is one such service with a good reputation.)

Securing permissions can take some time, possibly several months, so don't procrastinate. If you know that you want to use a particular excerpt or quote, determine if it requires permission and then get the ball rolling as soon as possible. You should also be prepared to pay a fee for the permission and for the possibility of your request being rejected. If your permission request is rejected, you must remove the material. If that means a major rewrite, you will want a significant amount of lead time so that you are not delaying publication. Fees can range from free to a thousand dollars or more; you may be able to negotiate with your publisher (if you have one) regarding who covers the expense.

To request permission, start by finding out who owns the copyright. If you are excerpting from a print source, the publisher's website may have a standard form and instructions for you to use. In general, these forms want to know exactly what material you are asking to quote, what your work is, how many copies will be printed, and where it will be distributed. If no form is provided, you can create your own. For all types of source material, be sure you are requesting permission from the right person or entity and that you know what kind of permission you need. For example, do you need print rights, electronic rights, or both? Do you need North America and Canada rights or world rights? Get the details worked out before you begin the process. (I won't get into all the different kinds of rights and licenses, as it is too big of a topic for this book; for an in-depth discussion, I recommend chapter 4 of *The Chicago Manual of Style*.)

This may all sound very tiresome, but the reality is, it's more than possible to receive permission for a well-known quote in a timely manner and for a reasonable fee. I recall working on one book that quoted Cyndi Lauper's "Girls Just Want to Have Fun." The permission was for world rights and cost only a hundred dollars. In this case, and many other cases as well, it was more important to the copyright holder that permission be obtained than to get a lot of money for that use.

Your DE can help you determine what needs permission and what doesn't. However, he or she is not likely to get in the middle of the permissions process. That will be up to you. Get started early so that you are not faced with delays.

Mapping Out Your Road to Success

Have a vision for your book that includes the audience, format, and tone.

Get involved with your target audience to learn as much as you can about them.

Keep the lines of communication open with your developmental editor.

Prepare to take your manuscript apart and put it back together in an even stronger form.

4
Cleaning Up Your Manuscript
Copyediting and Query Resolution

ongratulations! You have reached a major milestone on the road to a published book. Your completed manuscript, with its solid beginning, middle, and end, is ready for copyediting! While not all manuscripts will undergo development, every aspiring author should be prepared to go through this stage of editing. For many, the copyeditor is the first professional reader of the manuscript, and he or she is virtually guaranteed to discover problems that you missed. If you want to sell books, you need the safety net a copyeditor provides.

Copyeditors, also called CEs or line editors, focus on smaller issues than a developmental editor will have. Whereas DEs often take apart a manuscript and put it back together in a streamlined, orderly fashion, CEs look at the text line by line and paragraph by paragraph. Whether or not you will work directly with a copyeditor or through an intermediary depends on who is publishing your book. Some traditional publishers rely on the production editor, the point person in the production department who acts as a liaison to the vendors, to communicate with the copyeditor. (The role of the production editor is covered in more detail later in this chapter.)

Copyediting is an essential step for every book. Get your manuscript in tip-top shape now to avoid costly changes later in the process.

Others, notably academic presses, arrange for the copyeditor and author to work together, without an intermediary. In both cases, the publishing house hires and pays for the editing. In the third scenario, in which you are the publisher, you will hire and pay for the copyeditor yourself. Although professional copyediting takes time and money, by having your book copyedited before it is published, you are saving yourself the time, money, and embarrassment that you would pay if these errors were not corrected.

Depending on the length of your manuscript and the level of copyediting you need, you can expect to spend three to eight weeks in copyediting, with another two to four weeks for your review of the edited manuscript (called query resolution). A good guide is to allow one week for every seventy-five to one hundred manuscript pages—Times New Roman, 12-point font, double-spaced. Fees for freelance copyeditors range from $15 to $45 an hour. The rate is based largely on how complex or how technical the manuscript is, how messy it is, and whether it is fiction or nonfiction, with certain industries charging more than others. However, as with most things, you usually get what you pay for. The Potholes at the end of this chapter, "Stay Organized While You Research" and "Revise Your Manuscript One Last Time," highlight two sizable areas where authors can save themselves money by supplying the copyeditor with a manuscript with as few errors as possible.

WHAT YOU CAN EXPECT FROM YOUR COPYEDITOR

Copyeditors tend to be practical, straightforward people, and that's generally the approach they take to editing. Your CE will be reading the manuscript with the intent of cleaning up errors of punctuation, grammar, syntax, and word choice. That means correcting comma errors, fixing such problems as dangling or misplaced modifiers, rewriting convoluted sentences, and replacing words that have been used incorrectly.

CEs also read for flow and style. Correcting flow means fixing or querying transition problems, rearranging paragraphs if needed, and adjusting sentences so that one thought flows naturally from the one before it. Style refers to either the house style, if the book is published through a press, or an agreed-on style for self-publishers. Quite often editing for style means selecting one of two equally valid options, and it ensures consistency throughout the manuscript. Most trade books follow *The Chicago Manual of Style*, although there are plenty of others to choose from. If you hire a copyeditor, be sure he or she is familiar with this style guide or the guide of your choice. Points of style to keep in mind include whether or not to spell out numbers between ten and one hundred, whether or not to use the serial comma (i.e., the comma before the conjunction in a list of three or more items), and the spelling or capitalization of specific terms related to your field or, in the case of fiction, created universe. Traditional publishers will have a stable of freelancers who are familiar with their house style. Self-publishers should plan to discuss which style to use with their copyeditor before editing begins.

Finally, CEs read for sense and consistency. Sense, of course, means that what you are trying to say is what you actually are saying with the words you have chosen and that your plot or argument—whatever it may be—stands up to reasonable evaluation. Consistency covers a range of problem areas, from consistent spelling and treatment of special terms to consistent characterization and time line in a novel.

Inside Tip
The design for your book can be created from the unedited manuscript. If you are self-publishing, arrange with your designer to start the design process before the copyediting is complete. See Chapter 5 for details.

All of these changes, from grammar and punctuation to sense and consistency, are key in getting your book ready for publication. To find out whether editing, or a lack of it, affects sales, you need only to read reviews on Amazon to see that readers do notice and will deter others from buying books that contain these basic errors. In your quest for a high-quality book that sells, copyediting is essential.

Your copyeditor will also be on the lookout for passages that may require permission. Ideally you have already secured permission for long excerpts or any quotes from poetry and music. Those who worked with a developmental editor have probably at least begun this long process. If not, you will be asked to start now or else rework the text to eliminate the material requiring permission.

Writers of fiction and creative nonfiction may find the copyediting they receive to be much lighter than what a business, sports, or self-help author may experience. This is due to the creative nature of the work. These writers will still find plenty of changes to grammar and punctuation when clarity is at stake, but allowances are made for the author's voice and the voice of the characters. Some authors are concerned that a copyeditor will change dialogue from pidgin to standard English, for example, or otherwise take out the flavor of a character's way of speaking. Generally, these fears are unfounded. Good copyeditors understand the difference between what is intentionally incorrect and what is a mistake on the part of the author. And if it is not apparent, the CE will ask for clarification. For those who are self-publishing, a sample edit from your prospective copyeditor will allow you to determine whether he or she will change the voice of your characters.

As mentioned in the previous chapter, editing can be an emotional experience. Do your best not to take it personally when the CE changes your words. If you didn't go through development, it's possible that the CE has made significant changes: moving paragraphs, rewriting sentences, and adding transitions. If this gets

A Copyeditor Is Not a Fact-Checker

Although copyeditors will look up suspect words in the dictionary and check names and facts that strike them as incorrect, do not rely on your copyeditor to fact-check the entire manuscript. Besides the fact that vetting an entire manuscript takes precious time away from editing, copyeditors do not have the same resources as a dedicated fact-checker does. When it comes to your book, supplying accurate information is up to you. If you do not want to spend your time double-checking the spelling of place names, the dates of specific events, or quotes from famous speeches, you can hire the services of a fact-checker. Let your copyeditor concentrate on editing. In the end, you will get a much better product.

your ire up, be sure to go through the manuscript a second time before returning it, so that you can temper your angry notes to the copyeditor. If you are working with a production editor, or PE, remember that the PE is not the person who made these changes and therefore should not be the target of your hurt feelings. All in all, publishing a book requires a thick skin; use yours now.

It bears noting that for traditionally published authors, the copyediting stage is often your last chance to make major changes to the manuscript. If you went through development already or performed the tasks outlined in the Potholes for Chapters 1–3, as well as the two at the end of this chapter, you should have a minimum of large changes to make. Even still, consider any global changes as well as the smaller points you want to fix when reviewing the copyediting. As I told countless authors when I worked in-house, "Making changes later in the process is costly and time-consuming." If you don't make the changes now, they likely will not be made at all.

WHAT YOUR COPYEDITOR EXPECTS FROM YOU

Like most publishing professionals, copyeditors expect their authors to be respectful, flexible, and timely. The best authors to work with are those who understand that editors are working on more than one project at a time, respect that CEs are experts at what they do, and return the manuscript on time. The authors that CEs dread working with are those who call every day with questions instead of compiling their questions over a few days to be answered systematically, become rude or offended when the copyeditor changes something in the text, and are late (without notice) returning the edited and reviewed manuscript.

The tasks of a copyeditor are varied. Often they require knowledge of obscure grammar rules or specific preferences of a publishing house. Before getting up in arms about changes to your manuscript, consider that this one change to your manuscript may be a grammar rule that you are not familiar with. Ask about the changes you don't like or don't understand. Copyeditors do not expect you to know everything about writing, and most are happy to explain why they did what they did. But when a manuscript is returned with angry messages such as "Wrong!!" or "Stop changing my text!!" the author's welcome is soon worn out. I was recently scolded by an author when I changed "just desserts" to "just deserts." The author was furious. How could I introduce such an obvious error? Of course, the author didn't understand that the meaning of the phrase is not "only sweets" but "what you justly deserve." The in-house production editor said to let the author have his way, so I left the error. In that way, you could say the author got his just deserts for being rude. Be respectful of your editors, and remember, it is through collaboration that you will get the best product.

Inside Tip

When you send your manuscript to the copyeditor, stop working in the files. There should be only one set of live files, so that all desired changes appear in the same document. Instead, keep a list of updates you wish to make, and insert them when you have received the edited manuscript from the copyeditor.

Your CE will also appreciate your timeliness in returning the edited manuscript. If you are going to miss your deadline, communicate that to your editor. If instead you simply stop returning phone calls and e-mails as soon as your deadline passes, you may find yourself on your editor's bad side—whatever kind of editor you are working with. (This is particularly galling with authors who have been demanding of the editor's time up to this point.) It can be embarrassing when you don't do what you said you would do, and your CE may be a little bugged to hear that he or she has to adjust his or her schedule, but not as much as if he or she has to leave multiple messages trying to track you down.

Similarly, do not lie to your editor about when you have sent a manuscript. This may sound silly, but it happens with some regularity. When I was a new editor working in-house, I told a senior editor that I didn't know what happened; the author said she had sent the manuscript and it would arrive that day, but no package had arrived. Where could it be? "She probably didn't send the package," the experienced editor advised. "Give her a call." Sure enough, the author had *intended* to send the manuscript but hadn't quite finished her review. This was not my last brush with authors saying what they thought I wanted to hear, and it was frustrating every time. Bottom line: Communication is key to a good working relationship. Be respectful and take care not to leave your editor stranded.

In some instances, you may strongly disagree with your copyeditor. If you have reason to believe that the CE has introduced errors, missed many errors, or meddled unnecessarily with the text, you do have recourse. Traditionally published authors can bring the matter to the attention of the acquisitions editor or production editor. He or she will review the copyeditor's work and help find a solution. Self-publishers need to be their own advocates. Protect yourself by following the guidance in the sidebar "5 Steps to Hiring a Freelance Editor" in Chapter 3. If you get burned by a bad CE, you may be able to have your money refunded or you may just have to find a new editor. Building a reliable and good publishing team is one of the many challenges of self-publishing. No matter what, try to maintain a level of professionalism as you get your problems sorted out.

Besides being professional, there is another reason to maintain a good relationship with your CE: your work with this person does not necessarily end after you have reviewed the manuscript. There is still manuscript cleanup to navigate, in which the editor reviews the changes you made during query resolution, ensures you have answered all of the queries, then calls you with follow-up questions. With a traditional publishing house, either the production editor or the CE will fulfill these duties. If you are self-publishing, it's possible you will handle manuscript cleanup yourself, or you may have the freelance CE complete this step for you. We will talk more about manuscript cleanup in the following section.

ROADSIDE ASSISTANT

Kathy Clayton
Copyeditor and proofreader

Kathy Clayton has worked in the publishing industry for nearly twenty years. She started her career with four years at Harcourt College Publishers, first as an editorial assistant and later as a project editor, where she says she "discovered the joys of project management, copyediting, and proofreading." Later she worked as a project editor for McGraw-Hill and used her spare time to copyedit and proofread on a freelance basis. Kathy's other experience includes being the first managing editor for Texas Tech University Press and managing editor for *Texas EMS Magazine*. In 2014, Kathy launched Greenbelt Editing Services, where she provides copyediting, proofreading, and editorial project management.

As a copyeditor, what do you expect from an author in the way of a good working relationship?
A good working relationship with an author is just that—a relationship. The first thing I like to do is establish a comfortable level of communication. Then I try to convey a sense of teamwork between me, the author, and anyone else involved in the book's production. We are all working together to make the book the very best it can be, which means some back and forth to find the best solutions to each query and challenge. And a little patience with each other never hurts either. Whether it's scheduling, or researching references, or drilling down to the perfect phrase in the perfect spot, a good relationship with the author is the foundation for the whole copyediting process.

What advice do you have for new authors?
A new author needs one thing: patience. No matter what publishing route an author chooses, it will almost certainly take longer than expected to go from "final" manuscript to a book. Starting from there, then you should remember to have fun while you are working your way through all the steps. Hopefully the book started with a love of the topic, then you share it with professionals who love to do the work of book production, and then everyone brings the book itself to its fullest potential. What's not to enjoy?

What are some of the common mistakes you've seen as a copyeditor?
Common mistakes are hard to pin down. Every book is different, every writer is different, and every editor will see different ways

to improve a manuscript. Since you probably have access to a spell-checker, you can spend more time looking at other aspects of a book before you send it to a copyeditor. Poor organization is one of the biggest challenges we encounter. We have to know what you intend to say before we can help you say it best. That applies to everything from a single sentence to the entire book. An outline is one of the fastest ways to avoid organization mistakes. But really, it's the mistakes a copyeditor is there to fix, so we are excited to encounter new ones with each new project.

Can you share a best or worst author experience?
It seems like every experience with an author has a little bit of the "best" and a little bit of the "worst." As a copyeditor, I've had generally good luck with authors, but during my time as a production editor for a large publishing company, I encountered some unique characters. One of my favorites was a husband-and-wife team trying to double the length of a sidebar very late in the production stage. As I was gently explaining that the costs related to that change made it prohibitive, the woman asked if they could pay for the change themselves. I said, "No, I've never been aware of that being a viable possibility." To which she replied, "Well, you've never worked with authors like *us* before, have you?" It still makes me giggle.

THE PROCESS

If you publish more than one book, you'll find that there are a number of ways the copyediting stage could proceed. Here I outline the most common scenarios and include copyediting, query resolution, and manuscript cleanup.

Traditional Publishing

As mentioned, different publishing houses handle the copyediting stage in different ways. Talk to your acquisitions editor to find out if you will be working directly with the copyeditor or if the production editor will be your intermediary.

If you are working with a production editor (PE), she will be your point person for the copyediting process. The PE will send the manuscript to the copyeditor and then receive the copyedited manuscript and review it before passing it on to you, the author. The PE is helpful for a few reasons. One, she will check that the copyeditor has done a satisfactory job and will answer any queries (i.e., questions) that she can before sending you the manuscript. The PE also acts as a buffer between you and the copyeditor, which helps to defuse the sometimes hurt or angry feelings that can arise at this stage.

If you are working directly with the copyeditor, you will receive the manuscript from her. The benefits of this method are that it speeds the process by eliminating the middleman and relieves the in-house editors of some time-consuming tasks. The downsides are that the copyeditor may have to go back to the in-house editor if there are any disputes, and you as author have one more person to coordinate with and one more personality to accommodate. When you receive the manuscript—most likely via e-mail, although some publishers do still send hard copy—you will be given instructions on how to review the changes, any pertinent notes about the editing, and a deadline for returning the reviewed manuscript. If you did not go through development, you may have to learn Track Changes in Microsoft Word so that you can work through the editing.

Read through the CE's changes carefully to make sure your meaning is intact. The CE will have inserted queries for you, either directly in the text or as a comment. Answer these queries as completely as possible. If you are unclear as to what the editor is asking, don't just guess or type, "I don't understand." Find out so that you can answer it appropriately. Should the CE have made a change you don't like, you can either keep the text as you had it or make a different change that solves the problem. Generally the latter approach is best, since the copyeditor clearly thought there was a problem and other readers are likely to feel the same. If you think your CE has made an error, either fix it or discuss it with her.

The Compatible Copyeditor Conundrum

If you have the option of choosing your own copyeditor, be sure to choose someone who understands what you want out of the editing. Sometimes even good editors aren't the right editor for you. And it can be either side that makes this determination. A few years back a young woman contacted me and said she was looking for a copyeditor. She had tried a few others but hadn't found anyone she liked. She agreed to send a sample of the manuscript so that I could show her what kind of editing I do, and then we could go from there.

When I received the manuscript file, the author had made a note that she had a particular style that she didn't want changed. She didn't tell me what the style was; I was left to figure it out for myself. I was intrigued. As I read through the sample, I found the writing to be clean, with few grammatical or spelling errors, and the story was compelling. There was just one thing: I kept coming across alliteration in the middle of sentences. I changed a word or two to fix it the first time. The second time I made a change and explained that alliteration in prose can be distracting to the reader. By the third instance I realized that this was the style she had been talking about. I gave her my honest feedback—that she should remove the alliteration—and she found herself another editor, one who would support her style. It was the right decision for both of us.

Now, what happens after you review the copyediting? This stage is called manuscript cleanup. In manuscript cleanup, the CE or PE will review your changes and make sure you have answered all of the questions completely. The editor will also decide if all of your changes to the manuscript are correct per house style and the rules of grammar and punctuation. If there are any outstanding queries, you will receive a call or an e-mail asking you to answer those questions now. Should the editor decide not to make some of your changes—for instance, those that are not grammatically correct—you may or may not hear about it. If the change was small, it will almost certainly go without mention; larger edits that go unmade generally warrant a message from the PE or CE explaining why the changes were not implemented. You will go through as much back and forth as needed until all queries are answered to everyone's satisfaction. If you are thorough in your initial review, one round of discussions may be all that is needed.

Self-Publishing

The differences in the copyediting process for self-publishers come down to a matter of control and control's partner, responsibility. What is the self-publisher's role? First, you must find and hire your CE (see the sidebar "5 Steps to Hiring a Freelance Editor" in Chapter 3). Then you must discuss which style book you would like your CE to follow. Most authors skip this step, in which case your CE will use whatever style he is most familiar with, but it is better to make sure you are in agreement. At this time you can let your copyeditor know of any words or phrases that you prefer to be treated in a certain way—capitalized, italicized, hyphenated, and so forth—so that he isn't making changes you already know you won't accept. Next, you must (1) review the copyediting to ensure that it is up to your standards and (2) respond to any questions your CE may have.

> **Inside Tip**
>
> These days, 99 percent of copyediting is done electronically using the Track Changes function in Microsoft Word. Track Changes, while useful, can be difficult to follow at first, and you have several options for how to view the changes on-screen. If you have not done so already, take some time now to become familiar with this function.

At this point, the road splits on the process. Some freelance copyeditors working with self-publishers will perform the duties usually left to the production editor in a traditional publishing house. That includes reviewing your changes to make sure they are correct and consistent with the style of the book and ensuring that you have answered all of the queries completely. He will then make any formatting adjustments that are needed, accept all changes in the manuscript (remember that the editing was performed with Track Changes), and return to you a clean manuscript that you can send to your designer. There is

Three Ways Freelance Editors Are Paid

There are three main ways that a freelance editor may be paid—by the hour, by the page, and at a flat rate—and each has its pros and cons.

1. **By the hour:** This is the most common method for figuring fees. For the author, the pro here is that you are paying only for the actual time being spent. If your manuscript is in good shape with few errors, the number of hours will be smaller and you may be saving the most money this way. The downsides are that it makes budgeting more difficult (although your editor should give you an estimate before beginning work on the project) and you can't be certain that the editor actually spent as many hours as you are being billed for. Of course, if you are working with someone you trust, this last point should be a nonfactor.

2. **By the page:** The second most common way to figure fees is by the page. A standard manuscript page is defined by the Editorial Freelancers Association as 250 words. Divide your total word count by 250 and you know how many standard pages you have. Then multiply that number by the per-page rate and, voilà, you have your cost estimate for the project. The benefit here is that unless you add a significant amount of text, you know in advance how much the editing will cost you. The downside is that if your manuscript is clean, you may be overpaying. Of course, if your manuscript needs a lot of work, you may be underpaying. That uncertainty is the trade-off for having a set budget.

3. **Flat rate:** Paying a flat rate is the least common and the riskiest method. Normally this happens when a writer approaches an editor with a set amount of money he or she is willing to spend. The editor then decides if the project is worth that amount of money. The pro, again, is that the author has control over the budget. The con is that most of the time the flat rate is below a normal pay scale, and typically the editors who will agree to it are novices. You may find someone who is very good and willing to take on the project just because he or she has the time or is feeling generous; or you may discover that the old adage is true and you get what you pay for.

usually an additional charge for this service; however, it is a good way to ensure that your manuscript is in the best possible shape before it is typeset. If you choose not to pay for this service, or if your CE does not offer it, the responsibility falls to you to make sure that no new errors have been introduced and that the file is in good condition for your designer.

Your final responsibility is to pay your editor.

− − − − − −

Copyediting is an important step that all authors should go through to ensure that they are producing a work of the highest quality. Having a stranger pick apart your manuscript can be a great learning experience as well, not only in regards to your writing, but also in regards to your character. How well *do* you handle criticism? The good news is that copyediting is a fairly short stint on the road to a published book. When the editing is complete, you'll be ready to send it to the designer!

AVOIDING THE POTHOLE

Stay Organized While You Research

As part of the editing process, your copyeditor will do some light fact-checking and thoroughly edit any resources or reference sections found in your book. On occasion, major problems may be uncovered during this stage when it becomes clear that the author has not done everything he or she needed to do with the research for the book. These problems range from incomplete information in the references to factual errors to full-blown plagiarism. Although the copyeditor may be the one who highlights such issues, it is incumbent upon the author to fix them. On one hand, a book that is published without rectifying such errors opens the author up to public embarrassment and, potentially, legal action. On the other hand, a book that boasts good research is more desirable to readers, who expect and enjoy a well-cared-for manuscript. When you take the time to perform thorough research and keep good notes, you protect your reputation while also shoring up the marketability of your book.

The demands of research can vary significantly for nonfiction and fiction works. Let's take each genre in turn to see what you can expect and what is expected of you in this sometimes nebulous area.

NONFICTION RESEARCH REQUIREMENTS

It should be fairly obvious how proper research affects the quality of a nonfiction book. To maintain credibility as an author and sell the most books, you have to have your facts straight, and creative nonfiction is no exception. A guidebook that gives wrong contact information for the hotels it lists will receive harsh reviews online. A baseball biography that claims Babe Ruth, the most famous left-handed pitcher in the game, was right-handed will be laughed out of the bookstore (true story: I actually caught this mistake in a book I edited). If you're lucky, your editor will notice these kinds of errors, but you can't take that risk. Instead, take pride in your work and ensure that your manuscript has been thoroughly vetted. The stronger your research, the more marketable your book becomes.

But there's more. Beyond having your facts in order, you must also document where you found this information. You will likely be called on to supply source information, whether in a notes section, a reference list, or a list of resources for the reader. Keep copious notes and stay organized while you write so that you do not have to retrace your steps.

If you haven't had to document your research in a while, you may not remember what data you need to provide. Although different types of publications use different formats for their notes and references, recording the following information for each source will generally cover your needs:

◆ **Books:** author or editor, book title, city of publication, publisher, year, and page numbers for quotes

◆ **Chapters in books:** chapter author, chapter title, book editor, book title, city of publication, publisher, year, and page numbers for chapter

◆ **Journals:** author, article title, journal title, volume number, issue number, year, and page numbers

◆ **Newspaper articles:** author, article title, newspaper title, city (if not obvious), and date of publication; page numbers are not needed

◆ **Web pages:** author, title of web page, name of website (company or organization that runs the site), date of publication, and web address

For sources that don't fall into these categories, record the information that most closely aligns with your source. If any of the information is unavailable—for example, not all web pages have authors—make a note that there is no author so that you can easily answer that question when it comes back to you.

A Unique Kind of Nonfiction: The Memoir

Memoirs are generally understood to be one person's recollections of events as they pertain to that person. A certain amount of leeway is granted to these books regarding strict adherence to the facts, and often the writer will add a note to the reader stating that these are the facts *as they have been recalled by the author*. However, even memoirists do well to fact-check their manuscripts. I have edited not one but two memoirs—traditionally published—in which the names of at least fifty people were misspelled in the manuscript. One book, about a former movie star, also had incorrect film titles and shooting locations. The writers of these books assumed someone else would perform the unappetizing task of searching out the correct spellings, while they concerned themselves only with the writing. They were taking a big risk. What if those errors had made it into the published book? Both the author and the publisher would have been thoroughly embarrassed. You can expect editors to do limited fact-checking, but, ultimately, it is up to you to ensure the accuracy of your manuscript. If you do not wish to fact-check your work, you can hire someone specifically for that task.

Although you may find it tedious, tracking all of your sources as you gather information will save you time that otherwise would be spent hunting down page numbers and names of publishers later. It saves you money, too, as you don't have to pay an editor to spend the time to look up or query all of that missing information. Good organization also comes in handy when you want to write a follow-up book or a revised edition. Keep good files and you have saved yourself a few steps toward your next book.

FICTION RESEARCH REQUIREMENTS

Research for fiction writing might seem of lesser importance to you than that for nonfiction, but your readers and your agent or publisher (if you have one) will beg to differ. Although you are

creating a world of your own, it must still be based in some reality. If you stray from what your readers know to be true, that must be explained in some way in the narrative. Regarding historical events in fiction, it is acceptable, maybe even preferable, that you add details, characters, and dialogue. But for authenticity, you must get the big picture right. Do not fudge the facts just because you don't feel like looking them up.

Let me illustrate my point with an example. A very memorable researching problem once came up in a novel set in the 1940s. The author was describing a flashback in which the main character remembered Franklin D. Roosevelt's "Day of Infamy" speech as it aired on the radio. The problem arose when the author chose to pull out snippets of the speech as if the main character were hearing it for the first time. This was a nice touch to add authenticity for the reader, except that I was pretty sure the phrases she quoted were never spoken. To verify this, I searched online for a transcript of the speech, and, wouldn't you know it, the entire transcript came up. The phrases the author had chosen—"Day of infamy," "Japan bombed Pearl Harbor," and others—were nowhere in the speech. It took me less than five minutes to discover this. If the book had gone to press with such errors (and it was being self-published so I was the only one who might have caught them), the readers of this book would not have been happy. Instead of adding authenticity as the author had intended, she would have undermined her credibility.

It is possible to change some details of history, as long as you take the proper care with the material. In the bestseller *The Help* by Kathryn Stockett, the author includes a note in the acknowledgments at the back of the book that reads: "I took liberties with time, using the song 'The Times They Are A-Changin',' even though it was not released until 1964, and Shake 'n Bake, which did not hit the shelves until 1965." This was a simple way for Stockett to acknowledge that she had manipulated time because she felt it was appropriate for her intentions in the book. Readers will forgive this kind of bending of facts when it is done with care. Sloppy errors, on the other hand, will be noticed and will dismay your readers.

PLAGIARISM: A QUESTION OF INTEGRITY

As an editor, and one who enjoys seeing writing projects done right, I have become passionate about fighting plagiarism. I have learned over the years that for as rampant as plagiarism is (and it seems to be more prevalent than ever), it's not that difficult to avoid and it seems most people who plagiarize do so out of laziness. For me it has become the ultimate sign of authors' lack of respect for their work and their readers.

In some cases I do believe that there was just a misunderstanding. Either the author forgot to put in the source information or else he or she didn't know the rules governing plagiarism. For the former group, there's not much to be said except try to stay on top of your sourcing and don't take shortcuts. For the latter group, I outline in this section some of the more common plagiarism pitfalls authors fall into as well as how they are caught. As a professional writer, you can use this information to protect your work and your reputation.

Cut and Paste

To me, the most offensive kind of plagiarism is the cut-and-paste method. This is where whole sentences and sometimes whole paragraphs are taken verbatim from another source with no citation or mention whatsoever of the original source. (Even more galling is when the author has left in the hyperlinks and footnote markers from the original source!) Surprisingly enough, this seems to be the most common form of plagiarism and comes up in every kind of writing. How does this happen? I believe there are two routes. One is that the author cuts and pastes the material from an online source intending to use the information in a rewritten format, but he or she then neglects to go back and do the rewriting. The other is that the author has not taken the time to synthesize the material—read it, digest it, and write it in his or her own words—before using it in the book. Instead, the author took a shortcut, possibly assuming he or she couldn't have said it better and probably counting on no one finding out.

Now, how is this type of plagiarism discovered? Every author has a specific writing style that comes through to readers. You use certain words and sentence constructions; you write with a distinct tone—friendly or formal or technical, for example. If a new writer with his or her own word choice and sentence structure is introduced, as when someone else's work is copied, a reader will quickly spot it. At that point all that reader has to do is a simple search of the Internet to reveal the true source of the material. As a copyeditor I have made this discovery many times, and it is always embarrassing. I must now tell the author that I know he or she cheated, and the author must now own up to it and fix the problem. That is a scenario you should avoid at all costs.

Minor Revisions

This type of plagiarism is less often discovered, but it does get caught. In these cases the author has cut and pasted a paragraph or two from another source, changed a few words here and there, and passed it off as his or her own. The following is a real-life example from a novel I edited, shortened for the sake of brevity and with identifying markers removed.

Author's manuscript
The Mayor of [XXX] is the chief executive officer of the city government. The mayor has the responsibility of enforcing city ordinances and the power to either approve or veto mandates passed by the board of council members. Thirty-five individuals had held the office of mayor of [XXX], four of whom—John Powers, Francis Fletcher, Willy Garrett, and Vince Tucker—served non-consecutive terms.

Original source
The Mayor of the City of St. Louis is the chief executive officer of St. Louis' city government. The mayor has a duty to enforce city ordinances and the power to either approve or veto city ordinances passed by the board of aldermen.

Forty-five individuals have held the office of mayor of St. Louis, four of whom—William Carr Lane, John Fletcher Darby, John Wimer, and John How—served non-consecutive terms.

This is the kind of plagiarism your high school teachers warned you about. The trouble is, it is easy to convince yourself that with these minor changes, it is now your work. Unfortunately, you must do more. You must read the source, understand it, and restate it in your own words. If you want to be an author, you have to actually write the words that are published under your name or else seek permission. In this case, the passage was flagged for the author and the author rewrote it.

Improper Sourcing

A third kind of plagiarism, what I call improper sourcing, brings home the point that you must be very careful in your handling of material from other sources. In this category are the instances of a few sentences or, quite often, a list taken from another source, verbatim, with the source noted but without any quotation marks or visual cues to indicate exactly what is from the original source. Without the quotation marks or indentation for a block quote, your readers assume that you have taken ideas from another source but have not used any of the original author's words. Unlike the cut-and-paste and minor revisions categories, the original source is credited. That is a step in the right direction. But you must follow through and indicate for the reader what is a quote and what is not.

The root of this problem is not always known to me. Is it intentional or not? In the cases I've seen, it appears to be an oversight on the part of the author. That excuse, however, will not do you much good if you are sued. The lesson? Be especially careful when you use material from another source so that you do not wind up facing an accusation of plagiarism.

CASE STUDY: A BREACH OF RESEARCH ETHICS

One very good book I edited presented nearly every kind of research ethics breach there is, and it offers lessons for all writers. The problems stemmed from both the author's lack of knowledge of fair use and his resistance to writing new material.

This author, a nice fellow, contacted me about editing his historically important memoir. At the end of each chapter he had added historical background to give context to the story—an excellent concept. He sent me the manuscript for an initial evaluation.

The memoir portion of the manuscript was in great shape, but I was sorry to see that the historical notes were not so well prepared. Many of them were sourced to Wikipedia. Further, the citation information was often incomplete. For a book that was scheduled to be sold at the historical society, as this one was, that would not do. I outlined these problems for the author, telling him to find more reliable sources and include as much citation information as possible. He was open to and grateful for the feedback.

Several months later, the author contacted me again. He had revised the historical notes and was ready to proceed. As soon as I received the revised manuscript, I turned to the notes sections. Hooray! Very few if any Wikipedia references remained! Some of the publication information was incomplete and the formatting was off, but I could work with that. I agreed to begin editing.

Initially, everything looked great. But when I got deeper into the manuscript, at one point it struck me that a historical note I was reading might not have been written by this author. It was a little too formal, not the right vocabulary. So, I did a check online, and, sure enough, I found the passage verbatim. The author had not used quotation marks with these historical notes thus far; I had assumed the notes, some of which were several paragraphs, had been written in his words, synthesized from the source indicated with each note. Now, as I dug further, I saw that they weren't, and we had a problem. Yes, the source was given with the quote, but (1) without quotation marks there was no way for a reader to know that this was a quote and not the author's original writing, and

(2) even with the proper typographical notation indicating this was quoted material, some of the excerpts were far too long to fall under fair use. Permission would definitely be required.

Once again I went back to the author to let him know we had a serious problem. We had a few solutions to consider: add a lead-in and quotation marks to those notes that were short enough to fall under fair use; shorten, delete, or rewrite those that were too long to be fair use; or request permission to reprint the material. After discussing it with the author, we decided on a combination. I wrote the new lead-ins for the shorter quotes, and he shortened or deleted the quotes that were too long. The author also got lucky: one respected website granted permission for him to reprint as much of its material as he wanted, requiring only a citation. This was the best I could hope for, and I was glad we had come to a resolution. After a couple of weeks, it was all taken care of.

But just when I thought we were in the clear, another research-related problem came to light. Speaking with the author, I learned that he had shortened or edited some of the quotes *without noting his editorial changes.* Oh no! The author—any author, really—would be condemned for such abuse of an original source if the book went to press as it was. I explained that we could not change someone else's words without noting those changes. We needed ellipses for deleted material, brackets for added material. "Why?" he asked. My answer was simple: "Integrity. Integrity of the work you are citing and integrity of the work you are putting together." The author now had to reconstruct the original quotations, noting his editorial changes properly. Another week passed before we could finally complete the editing process.

Because this author did not know the rules of documentation, he had to thoroughly revise the historical notes three times before they were finally in a condition acceptable for publication. And that bar was set fairly low: we made sure only that he couldn't be sued. Had this author known the rules and taken more time up front to perform and present his research correctly, he would have saved many, many hours of work down the road, not to mention the cost of editing material that eventually would be replaced.

AVOIDING THE POTHOLE
Revise Your Manuscript One Last Time

Copyeditors are tasked with catching a wide range of errors. Spelling, grammar, punctuation, flow—these mistakes often require a second set of eyes to discover them. However, it is possible to alleviate some of your copyeditor's work, thereby saving you time and money, simply by performing one final revision. For authors seeking an agent or traditional publisher, this step will come before you submit your final manuscript. For self-publishers, it occurs immediately before you embark on the editing process. Carefully revising a manuscript demonstrates professionalism and competence on your part, and a well-crafted manuscript saves you time and money throughout the book production process.

We begin with an explanation of common errors found in all types of works, and then address considerations specific to fiction and nonfiction. Keep these points in mind as you read through your manuscript one last time.

> **Inside Tip**
>
> If you are self-publishing and know you want to produce an e-book, take a look at the formatting guidelines from the various e-book companies noted in Chapter 7. Then refer to this information as you prepare your manuscript. Doing so will help to cut down on the adjustments you need to make before uploading your file for conversion to e-book.

WHAT TO LOOK FOR

In crafting your manuscript you have strengthened your knowledge of the market, implemented a marketing hook, and ensured details such as research and permissions are in order, all essential in creating a high-quality book. Now, before you go any further,

read through your manuscript to be certain you are hitting o
cylinders. Read for:

- Audience

- Tone

- Sense

- Flow

- Grammar

- Spelling

That's easy enough to say, but let's look at each of these areas in depth to find out what each entails.

Audience and tone, once you have defined for yourself what you want those to be, are tied closely to word choice and sentence structure. Although difficult to verbalize, they are often easy to hear. As you listen in your mind to the words you have written, can you envision your target audience following along? Are you consistently striking the tone you have been striving for: authoritative, friendly, or humorous? Continue to ask yourself this question throughout your reading. Do your best to maintain a consistent voice for the duration of the book. There are no rigid rules on how to accomplish this. You must rely on your ear to catch any vagaries.

Checking for sense may seem obvious. Does what you wrote make sense to the reader? However, when you are the writer and you know exactly what you mean, it can be difficult to recognize what does and does not come across. This is one of the big reasons we have copyeditors and proofreaders. For now, do what you can. Set the manuscript aside for a few days. Then take your time to ensure that you are not making assumptions about what your reader already understands to be true. If you aren't sure whether your meaning is coming through, ask someone else to read the passage and tell you what it means. Your intent may be perfectly clear, or you may find you have left out an important word or bit of information that you must now work into the text.

Flow is another aspect without rigid rules. This element is all about transitions. Are your chapters transitioning smoothly from one to the next? Are paragraphs in the best order? Are your sentences flowing together nicely to make your meaning clear? Some authors seem to be opposed to conjunctions (you know, the small words that join words, thoughts, and clauses). At one time it was taboo to start a sentence with *and, or, nor, but,* or *yet.* For some writers that rule seems to have been expanded to include *however, although,* and the other subordinating conjunctions. But the taboo has fallen by the wayside, and thank goodness. Conjunctions are essential in letting your reader know how one idea relates to another, and sometimes it only makes sense to begin a sentence with one. Of course, you don't have to start your sentences that way. Just be sure that you are using enough conjunctions and transitional phrases so that your readers can follow your train of thought.

For some, more difficult than recognizing problems of sense and flow or keeping a consistent voice is ensuring correct spelling and grammar. Not everyone is a good speller or a grammarian. However, as the author you must do your best. Don't simply run

Words of Wisdom

Need some guidance on how to tell if your book is any good? Now a literary agent and publishing consultant, Jane von Mehren is a former senior vice president and publisher of the Trade Paperbacks department at Random House. In her essay in *Editors on Editing,* titled "What Editors Look for in a Query Letter, Proposal, and Manuscript," she offers this poignant advice:

Ask yourself: Is my plot or argument persuasive; is it well executed; does each scene, character, conversation, and idea make an important and effective contribution to the work; is it original; will it keep people outside of my family and closest friends reading through the last page?

Isn't That What Editors Are For?

Many authors are tempted to skip this final revision. Why take the time to do something you or the publisher is going to hire someone else to do later? The reason is threefold:

1. More than likely your copyeditor will have plenty to review and correct without the small (or large) changes you make now. You simply can't perfect a manuscript on your own.
2. The cleaner your manuscript is, the fewer hours your copyeditor will need to spend fixing problems you could have fixed yourself. Fewer hours of work for the copyeditor mean less expense for you.
3. If you are reaching out to agents and publishers, the more polished your manuscript the better your chances of being accepted.

spell-check, accept all of its suggestions, and call it good. The dictionaries that word-processing programs employ are dubious at best. Instead, when spell-check highlights a word you aren't sure about, get out your dictionary or find a good one online (most US publishers use *Merriam-Webster's*) and look it up. For grammar, I suggest turning to *The Elements of Style* by Strunk and White. This slim volume covers everything you need to know for clean, clear, and concise writing. Other, more involved grammar and style books, such as *The Chicago Manual of Style* or *MLA Style Manual and Guide to Scholarly Publishing*, will also help, but it's hard to beat the ease and accessibility of *Elements*, which offers *dos* and *don'ts* for nearly every instance of grammar and does so in less than a hundred pages.

Beyond using the right resources, the key to good self-editing is distance. If you attempt to make these edits the day after you type "The End," you will have a difficult time separating what you meant to write from what you actually wrote. So take at least a week off—a month if possible—then make your final pass. You may be surprised at the errors you uncover.

Finally, do not let yourself off the hook when you come across a problem area. I believe every writer does this to some extent. As you're reading along, something odd strikes your ear. It may be in the sentence you have restructured three times already or perhaps it is a new sore spot. But instead of stopping and taking another look, you breeze past it, thinking it's fine as is and no one else will notice. Unfortunately, someone always notices. Do what you can now to make sure those problem areas are smoothed over before handing your manuscript to a professional editor.

CONSIDERATIONS FOR FICTION WRITERS

What I have outlined in the preceding section applies to all types of writing, but fiction adds a handful of areas that need specific attention, including plot, characterization, and time lines. It may be necessary to do another read-through for these issues alone.

The overarching challenge that all three of these elements pose is consistency. Let's take plot first. Ask yourself, are there holes or loose ends in the plotline? Is there a plot point that at one time you planned to take somewhere but have since left without conclusion? Does the action in one part of your book contradict or, more often, preclude something that occurs later in the manuscript? If you outlined your plot at the start, your notations may clue you in to any ends left dangling. Your copyeditor will be on the lookout for these vagaries; if you can address them before going into production, your CE will be able to focus on other aspects of the book.

Consistent characterization requires writers to keep a permanent picture in their minds of the person they are describing. Problems arise when that picture changes, often when it becomes convenient to the plot for a particular character to act one way in one situation and in an opposing way in a later but similar situation. If you have a woman who is supposed to be a longtime police officer, for instance, it will not do to have her come across as naive or scandalized when she learns of some heinous crime in her neighborhood. People do behave differently in various situations—we may be shy with some people and outspoken with

others, for example—but those vacillations must be explained through descriptions of the characters and the scenes. Watch out for instances where you have forgotten who your character is or where you have made concessions just to fit your plot. Your reader requires that you either adjust the plot or explain this new behavior.

Finally, keep track of the time line you have set your plot against. If your story includes flashbacks or a nonlinear construct, you must be very careful. Readers will notice if your main character is said to be in two places at once or to know information that he or she could not have learned in the amount of time said to have passed. Writing up a detailed time line for yourself will help you ensure that all of the pieces of the puzzle are fitting into place.

CONSIDERATIONS FOR NONFICTION WRITERS

Most nonfiction has some amount of front and back matter, and many new writers are unaware of the conventions that are attached to these elements. Getting these pieces right will help you wash off the amateur stink you may be carrying. The appearance of professionalism you will gain can go a long way in selling books to readers, agents, and publishers.

Front Matter

Front matter refers to all of the material that comes before chapter 1. Common elements include the title page, copyright page, dedication, epigraph, table of contents, foreword, preface, acknowledgments, and introduction. Note the order in which those elements are listed, for that is how your manuscript should be ordered. (If you have acknowledgments, those can go either before the introduction or in the back matter.) You may not have a copyright page yet, and if you are being published by someone else you may be asked to hold off on the introduction, depending on your editor,

but the other pieces can be in place, and you may wish to include a placeholder for anything that is still to come.

These sections of the book require much the same attention as the rest of the manuscript as far as revising is concerned. What I want to highlight here are the distinctions between three of the front matter elements that new authors often confuse: the foreword, the preface, and the introduction. Knowing the differences will help you appear professional and polished, enhancing your marketability.

- A foreword is written by someone else as a kind of endorsement of the book. This is nice to have but not essential. If you know anyone with good credentials or name recognition, you may leverage that contact to help sell your book. You can remember where to place a foreword if you consider that the material not written by the author belongs farthest away from the author's own writing.

- A preface is written by the author. This should tell a little about you as the author and how you came to write this particular book. Keep the autobiographical information relevant to the book you are writing. Include a preface if knowing your approach to the subject will help your readers understand the contents of the book.

- An introduction offers material directly tied to the book. This is not the place to tell about yourself. That goes in the preface. Instead, tell readers what they will get out of your book. This can be a loose description or a chapter-by-chapter outline. Most nonfiction books benefit from an introduction, as it functions as marketing material for readers browsing your book as well as giving context for the reader.

It might seem silly to quibble over these differences, but I do believe it's important for writers to get them right. Readers have an expectation for the content of a section based on the heading at the top of the page, and when that content does not match their expectations, it can leave them dissatisfied or confused.

Making Sure the Art Program Is in Order

As you head into copyediting, your art program—that is, the photos and illustrations for your book along with accompanying legends or captions and credits—is probably still in flux. Large art programs can be unwieldy, and good organization is key. Take time to compare the images with the captions and credits to make sure they match. If something is still to come, whether that's a piece of art, a caption, or a credit line, make note of that in your art manuscript so that everyone is aware of the status.

Back Matter

Back matter, sometimes called end matter, refers to the appendixes, time line, notes, glossary, reference lists, resources, and index, among other potential elements, that appear at the end of a book. These pieces of the manuscript, once again listed in the generally accepted proper order, require a different kind of revision from what you will have performed for the rest of the book. With the exception of appendixes that are narrative, your concerns with back matter are not so much flow, sense, and grammar as completeness of information and, if possible, consistency in formatting of the material.

Endnotes and reference lists require extreme attention to detail. Completeness is essential so that your readers can retrace your work. Not all publishing houses (if you are going that way) will supply you with formatting guidelines, but for those that do, read and follow them to the best of your abilities. If you have not been given guidelines or are self-publishing, choose a style manual that is in keeping with your field. General-interest nonfiction books will most likely follow *The Chicago Manual of Style*. Academic books tend to follow either *Chicago* style or *MLA Style Manual and Guide to Scholarly Publishing* for their back matter. Other specific fields have their own guides. Particularly helpful for notes and reference lists, these guides can tell you what information to include and in what order to list it. For any other back matter pieces you have opted to include—resources, glossary, tabular material—strive for consistency.

Except for certain works of creative nonfiction, most nonfiction books also benefit from an index. The index is created not from the manuscript but from the typeset page proofs that the designer creates. Chapter 6 has more information on how to handle the index.

Mapping Out Your Road to Success

Handle material from other sources with respect, and fact-check your writing.

Save time and money by revising your manuscript carefully before sending it to the copyeditor.

Keep the lines of communication open between you and your copyeditor and/or production editor.

Review the copyediting closely and make any major changes now.

5

Making It Look Good
Design and Layout

For many authors, design and layout are the most fun parts of book production. You get to watch your manuscript transform from straight text into something that looks like an honest-to-goodness book. But it doesn't happen by magic. Great design requires a great designer.

You'll hear a number of names used for the person who designs and lays out a manuscript: designer, typesetter, compositor, layout artist. Although it is possible to have a separate layout artist, interior designer, and cover designer, more and more these jobs are all done by the same company, if not the same person. For simplicity, this chapter uses *designer* in all instances.

The design stage usually runs concurrent with copyediting, but it isn't until you have a final manuscript, after copyediting and query resolution are completed, that layout can begin. It is in layout that page proofs are created for the full manuscript. The design is decided based on just a portion of the unedited manuscript.

In traditional publishing, creating a design for your book is a truly collaborative process. You and the acquisitions edi-

Just as a professional-looking cover design is essential for your book to compete in the marketplace, a compelling interior design and smart layout complete the look of professionalism.

tor (AE) come up with some ideas, and the AE uses his or her expertise and knowledge of the market to guide the decisions. Your combined input is then given to the production editor, who coordinates with the designer to create a design that fits those requirements as well as certain house specifications. Then seemingly everyone in the publishing house reviews what the designer comes up with and makes changes until all parties are satisfied.

Self-publishers are on their own to navigate this process. Some opt to do the design themselves. Unless you are a book designer and layout artist by trade, this is probably a mistake. The one author I know who did her own design had a background in art, and she still wasn't entirely satisfied with the way her cover turned out. There are a lot of details to making a book look professional that you more than likely never noticed—because they were done correctly. When they are not done correctly, readers will assume this is not a top-quality book. Professional design, even more so than professional editing, is how you ensure that your book stands up to the competition.

Because traditionally published authors have limited interaction with designers, much of this chapter is geared toward the self-publisher. However, knowledge of the process, what to expect, and what is expected of you as the author will make this step easier no matter what path you are on. If you are unsure about which route you will take, the information presented here will help you make that critical decision. Finally, the Pothole for this chapter explores how to evaluate book designs and how to use design to its fullest potential in your book. Design is a great way to enhance the reading experience.

Finalizing a book design can take two to four weeks. Manuscript layout—when the designer takes your manuscript text and applies the agreed-on design—takes another two to four weeks, depending on the length and complexity of the book and your designer's schedule. Costs for interior design and layout range from $6 to $10 per page, plus a setup fee of between $100 and $200. Cover designs generally range from $600 to $1,200 but can go much higher if specialty artwork is required.

The Terminology of Design

You'll discover quite a number of new terms thrown around when discussing design, beginning with what name to call the person designing and laying out your book. Here's an overview:

Designer: The person who creates the interior and cover design for your book; also called *interior designer* or *cover designer*

Layout artist: The person who applies the interior design to your manuscript and lays out page proofs; also called *typesetter* or *compositor*

Page proofs: The pages of your book once the design has been applied and before it is bound; a *proofreader* reads page proofs for errors

Spread: Two facing pages

Signature: A group of printed sheets of paper that are folded and bound at the printer; one signature often equals sixteen or thirty-two pages

Bad breaks: End-of-line and page breaks that either look bad or make it difficult for the reader to follow the text

CMYK: The four colors used in color printing: cyan, magenta, yellow, and black

RGB: The three colors used by computer monitors: red, green, and blue

1-color: Black-and-white

2-color: Black-and-white plus an accent color

4-color: What the rest of us mean when we say "color"

JPEG, TIFF: The preferred file types for most artwork

Bleed: Where artwork or other design elements intentionally run off the page

Verso: The left-hand page of a book; the even-numbered pages

Recto: The right-hand page of a book; the odd-numbered pages

Folio: Page number; a *drop folio* is placed at the bottom of the page

Running head: The heading that runs across the top of a page; often author and book title (fiction) or book title and chapter title (nonfiction)

Thumb: The outside margin of a book page

Gutter: The inside margin, near the spine of the book

WHAT YOU CAN EXPECT FROM YOUR DESIGNER

Professional designers offer an expertise that most literary types don't have: they know what it takes to make a book visually appealing. That includes a wide range of aspects, from choosing appropriate artwork (photo or illustration), colors, and fonts for your subject area or genre to knowing the best spacing to use on chapter-opening pages and where to place the page numbers and running heads. Further, your designer will be able to locate the correct artwork and, if you are self-publishing, may be able to help you secure licenses for using the art. For the traditionally published author, the publishing house most often takes care of licensing.

You can also expect your designer to understand good layout principles. That means knowing how to "twin" pages—that is, make sure that the tops and bottoms of facing pages align—and fix bad breaks. It also includes making adjustments to spacing, hyphenation, and justification to ensure that the last page of a chapter has enough lines of text (at least six lines is optimal; four is passable) and that there are no blank right-hand pages.

When it comes to choosing the design for your book, your designer will do his or her best to represent your ideas. It is helpful if you have specific ideas to share, rather than vague notions, but also be sure to listen to your designer if he or she is gently nudging you in a certain direction. The designer may have reasons for his or her ideas that you aren't aware of, and, in my experience, if you don't ask your designer's opinion, you won't get it. The designer will give you what you asked for, even if it isn't his or her first choice.

If you are self-publishing, you will work directly with your designer to come up with design ideas that are appropriate for your book. Your designer will listen to your ideas and attempt to convey your vision for the book through the cover and interior designs.

Although you may use a different interior designer and cover designer, or possibly a template interior and a custom cover design

Inside Tip
At this stage self-publishers who will have a print edition need to coordinate with their printers on aspects of trim size, cover materials, paper, and print specifications. Be sure your designer has experience working with printers before you hire him or her.

E-Books and Design

The technology of e-books has altered some of the conventional wisdom about design. With an e-book, there is no set thumb or gutter margin, no bad page break. Any illustrations, charts, or graphs will "float" rather than being stable on the page. Often the manuscript won't even be imported into a specific design program but instead will be designed in Microsoft Word. Unless the book is also going to be printed, the designer will apply the style in Word and then focus on formatting the manuscript file to the specifications required by e-readers (Kindle, Nook, Kobo, and iPad being the most popular). With a traditional publishing house, this goes on behind the scenes and you don't have much to worry about. You should, however, double-check that the most up-to-date file is being used to make the e-book and not an older version of the manuscript that still contains errors.

With self-publishing, you will want to ensure that your designer has worked with e-books before and is able to meet the specifications of your chosen e-book company. If you are working with multiple e-book platforms—AZW or MOBI for Kindle; ePub for Nook, iPad, and others—you may need multiple files, each prepared to the specs of the individual platforms, or use an e-book company that can convert the file for you. Alert your designer right away if you plan to have an e-book.

E-books do not require a full cover, only a front cover and the marketing copy. Because there is no back cover, the front cover must do double-duty, often carrying the most powerful endorsement and any bursts noting special features. The front cover also must be legible when viewed as a 1-inch-by-2-inch thumbnail. Both self-publishers and traditional publishing houses must make these accommodations for books sold online.

from your designer, you will achieve a more seamless look if the same person does both designs. Template interiors work best with all-text books such as novels, where it is unlikely that a lot of adjustments will need to be made. Self-publishing advocate Joel Friedlander sells templates for Microsoft Word through his website (www.thebookdesigner.com), while some designers offer templates at a savings compared to a custom design.

Those working with traditional publishing houses should recall that although they have input on the cover and interior designs for their books, they very rarely get final approval. That means you can give your opinion, but you are not likely to get everything you want.

WHAT YOUR DESIGNER EXPECTS FROM YOU

As mentioned, authors who have signed with a traditional publishing house will have little direct contact with the designer. Therefore, designers do not have many expectations from these authors specifically. Nevertheless, for all authors, a good working relationship with a designer requires a collaborative mind-set.

Designers working with self-publishers expect their clients to have an opinion about what the design should be. If you have researched the competition ahead of time, you are in great shape, as you probably already have thoughts on what you like and what you don't. Designers are the creative minds, however, and do best with a little freedom. That is to say, if you let them, good designers will take your ideas, add a few of their own, and bring you two or three design options that look great and fit your needs. If you have not formulated your thoughts on how your book should look—for example, you have not researched the competition and therefore do not know what the conventions are for your genre—your designer will have to come up with something all on his or her own. This may work out great, but it also may happen that although you did not know how to *verbalize* what you like, you did indeed have an opinion, and the designer has missed the mark. This will result in many back-and-forths that could have been eliminated if you had done some research beforehand. Conversely, if you know precisely what you want, down to the last detail, you leave your designer with no room to be creative. You may get exactly what you want, but you lose the advantage of having hired an expert, and what you want may not be what is best for the marketability of the book. Looking through other books to find the designs you like may take a bit of time, but it's also a lot of fun. It means your idea for a book is getting closer to reality.

When it is time for layout, be organized. Your manuscript file should be clean and ready to go, and your artwork and captions should be numbered and organized. A "clean" manuscript is free of extra spaces between words or sentences, free of extra paragraph breaks, and free of extra tabs. The entire file is double-spaced and in one standard font, such as Times New Roman, Arial, or Courier New. All text is "normal"; there are no random style sheets applied via Microsoft Word. And any queries from the copyeditor have been removed, with all tracked changes accepted. If you supply your manuscript this way, the designer can focus on more important issues and you will receive your page proofs that much faster.

ROADSIDE ASSISTANT

Sue Knopf
Interior and cover designer

The owner of Graffolio, Sue Knopf has designed books since 1988 for publishing companies and self-publishers across the country. She is approaching retirement after designing and laying out (and sometimes editing) more than 300 books.

What do you expect from an author in the way of a good working relationship?

◆ Ask enough questions to understand the way the designer works, and make sure you understand how the designer charges and when payments are due.

◆ Tell the designer up front if you have to meet a certain deadline.

◆ With the designer, set a schedule describing when both you and the designer will have components finished.

◆ Collect questions and ask several at once rather than calling or e-mailing frequently with small questions.

What advice do you have for new authors?

♦ Start interviewing designers well before your manuscript is ready so that you can find one who you think you can work comfortably with and who also has time to do your project.

♦ When you're thinking about what you want your book's design to look like, go to a bookstore or library (or simply look on your own bookshelf) and examine books in your book's genre. See what you like or don't like. If you can photocopy some pages you like and send them to your designer, that will help. Your designer will probably ask you lots of questions about things you may never have thought about or noticed:

◇ What should chapter openings look like?

◇ Do you want all of your chapters to start on right-hand pages?

◇ What trim size will you use? If you're planning to use something other than standard 6 × 9, 5.5 × 8.5, or 8.5 × 11, talk to printers and see what sizes are economical to print.

♦ Be aware that the first proof of your book won't be perfect; you'll probably have to go through at least three proof stages before things are exactly as you want them.

♦ Be aware that you may have to make some compromises—for example, maybe you'd like your book to have at least two hundred pages and have a 6 × 9 trim size, but the only way to do this is to have type or margins larger than you think is attractive.

What are some of the common mistakes you've seen as a designer?

♦ Not getting started with the designer early enough in the process. Design work can be done before the manuscript is ready, but the final layout should wait until the manuscript has been finalized and edited and all other materials (photos, etc.) have been collected and marked.

- Not hiring a professional editor, proofreader, and (if needed) indexer.

- Not being realistic about the schedule. Allow time for design, layout of first proof, proofreading of first proof, creation of second proof and its proofreading, and final proof and proofreading. Add more time if you'll need an index or photography or other artwork.

- Not sharing the design with everyone you plan to accept advice from early in the design/layout process. I hate to hear, when I'm working on the second proof, "I just showed this to my friend Bob, and he thinks the type is too small. Can you make it larger?"

- Not providing all of the material at once, but sending things in piece by piece.

Can you share a best or worst author experience?
I'll share both!

Best: The manuscript was carefully edited. The materials for each chapter (a printout of the chapter's computer file and photos for me to scan) were in a manila envelope marked with the chapter number. The computer files were logically and consistently named with chapter numbers. The photos were marked on the back using a logical system—for example, the chapter 1 photos were numbered 1-1, 1-2, 1-3, and so on. Each photo number was penciled in on the manuscript page near where the photo should go.

Worst: One of the worst is happening right now. The photos are disorganized and in several locations; some are provided in two locations at different resolutions and with inconsistent numbering; some are missing; some are embedded in a Word file, requiring a conversion process. Not all of the photo locations are marked in the manuscript. There are two printed versions of the manuscript and neither is complete, so I have to refer to both of them. The computer file is a little different from either of the printouts. The schedule is ambitious.

THE PROCESS

Although they go hand in hand, design and layout are two distinct steps. In both stages, the traditionally published author is minimally involved. Self-publishers, conversely, take a leading role in both.

Traditional Publishing

The design process begins with the author and AE brainstorming ideas about the design. This discussion will include likes and dislikes as well as what is needed to fit in with—and stand out from—the competition. The results of this discussion are passed on to the production editor (PE; the in-house editor who shepherds projects from manuscript to book), who will guide the rest of the interior design process.

While the manuscript is out for copyediting, the production editor takes a copy of your original, unedited manuscript; applies design codes to the various type elements that stand out from the regular text, such as chapter titles, headings, and tables and boxes; flags examples of all of these elements; and sends that plus the AE's notes to the designer. The designer may also get some marketing materials so that she knows what angle to take with the design. Designers may work in-house, but more often they are hired as out-of-house vendors.

A couple of weeks later, the designer returns with a design sample—ten or so pages of text pulled from your manuscript and laid out in the design, often with some alternatives to choose from. This allows the AE, PE, managing editor, and in-house design specialist (if applicable) to review the design and make changes. Each of these people is looking for something different and will make comments and changes based on his or her area of expertise. The marked-up design sample is then returned to the designer, and a few days later a new design sample is sent around for review. At that point a few more changes may be noted, until all parties are satisfied. You as the author may or may not have input at this time.

By the time the copyedited manuscript is back from query resolution and has been cleaned up, the design will have been

The Interplay of Art and Design

Art-heavy books—that is, those with more than twenty or so illustrations, photos, charts, or line drawings—require a lot of manipulation during layout so that each photo or illustration lands near enough to the text that it belongs with. Sometimes the text may need to be rewritten or captions revised in order to accommodate all of the artwork.

In contrast, fiction and other all-text books require very little manipulation, as there are few special elements to disrupt the flow of regular text. This is one more reason why it is cheaper to make an all-text book when compared to one with many illustrations, an important consideration for both the traditionally published author and the self-publisher.

finalized, which is a good thing because it is now time to apply the design to the final manuscript. The designer takes the manuscript text, which up until now has been in Microsoft Word, and "pours" it into Quark or InDesign—the preferred design software for book publishers. The designer then manipulates any artwork, captions, sidebars, boxes, charts, headings, and text so that it looks nice on the page and meets the specifications set out by the publishing house.

When the designer finishes laying out the book, she delivers page proofs to the publishing house, either as printouts or as a PDF. A few checks by the PE—all pages are present and no glaring errors have been introduced—and your book is ready for the next step in book production: proofreading.

The cover design process starts the same way, with input from you and the AE, but for covers, the editorial board puts in its suggestions and makes changes. The board is made up of the publisher, other AEs, marketing and sales professionals, and the designers. They use their knowledge of the market and their subjective opinions to choose the best cover. The author is not usually consulted on the final cover, although you may be able to suggest some tweaks. Covers are usually decided before the manuscript is sent out for copyediting, or shortly thereafter.

Self-Publishing

The first step in the design process for a self-publisher is finding a qualified designer. Similar to finding a good editor, your best bet is to start with referrals from friends and trusted colleagues. If you are working with an editor you trust—the only kind of editor you should be working with—ask him or her for referrals. You may also check out the Artists and Art Services sections of *Literary Market Place* (www.literarymarketplace.com) or the freelancer database on the Editorial Freelancers Association website (www.the-efa.com), among other sources. Contact two or three designers so that you can get a feel for the range of design styles. Most designers have a portfolio available either on their business website or for viewing through another site. Review these portfolios, and then ask for a bid. When researching a designer, look for someone who has experience specifically with *book design*, as books require different knowledge from marketing materials, newsletters, and other publications. Your book designer may do these other projects as well, but not everyone who does newsletters will understand the ins and outs of book design.

When it comes to actually hiring someone, qualifications and expense often compete for highest priority. The tie-breaker may come down to whose style best fits your project. Particularly when you consider the importance of design to book sales, the designer whose qualifications and style meet your expectations may justify any added expense.

When you have located the designer of your choice, talk to him about your ideas and your budget. It is helpful if you can point to specific book designs that you like. Ideally, these books are in your genre, as different genres have different conventions, but that is not required. Your designer will then offer his ideas about what will work for your book, and, based on your conversation, he will create samples for the cover and the interior. Be critical of the design. If you're new to this, you might not entirely understand what you are looking at. Try comparing the design to a traditionally published book to see if it follows those conventions. Some generally accepted conventions for interior designs include the following:

- Chapter-opening pages should use drop folios or no page number.

- There should never be a running head on a chapter opener or blank page.

- If the headings and subheadings in your book are flush left, normally the text immediately below the heading should also be flush left.

- The body text should be justified left and right.

- There should be more space above a heading than below it.

- If there is space preceding a list, there should also be space after it; if there is no space above, then there should be little or no space below.

Look at these details in your sample and, if anything doesn't look right, either mark to have it changed or query your designer as to why he did it that way. The designer will make adjustments until you are satisfied with the final design.

You will also receive two or three samples for the cover. With cover designs, I recommend striving for simplicity. Now that a book is judged by the cover as it appears online, you need to ensure that the title is legible when viewed as an icon on a screen. Be wary of covers that are cluttered, difficult to read, or too literal a representation of the contents of your book.

As you are in charge of the schedule for your book, coordinating the completion of manuscript cleanup with completion of the interior design is a worthy challenge. No real harm comes from having a final manuscript before a final design, but if you have a publication date in mind, you may not want to lose this time. Conversely, if you finalize the design before the copyediting is complete,

Inside Tip

In *The Complete Guide to Self-Publishing*, authors Marilyn Ross and Sue Collier note, "Be sure your contract with the cover designer is 'work made for hire.'... You don't want your designer to own the rights to your cover." With a work made for hire, you have the freedom to use the cover image however you see fit. Of course, a credit to the designer on the copyright page is expected.

you may discover that new elements have been added or uncovered that were not included in the design. Generally this is an easy fix. Just be sure to alert your designer about any element—such as a new level of subhead, an extract, or a two-column list—that has not been designed.

How you send your materials to the designer is a big consideration. Your designer will most likely want to receive your manuscript all at once rather than in bits and pieces. (The exception may be sending front matter after the other parts of the manuscript, since front matter can be laid out separate from the other chapters.) Find out if your designer prefers to receive your manuscript broken into separate files for each chapter or as one complete document. Any artwork that is to appear in the book should be keyed to the text—that is, each photo, illustration, table, or chart should be given a number and you or your copyeditor should place notes in the text stating where each one should appear. The captions that go with the artwork also must be numbered, with the caption bearing the same number as the photo or illustration to which it belongs. Most likely you will want to keep the captions in their own document to be supplied separately from the text, but check with your designer to make sure this is OK.

Once you have the final manuscript file, you can send it to the designer, who will begin the layout process. When layout is complete, two to four weeks later, the designer will send to you page proofs, either in hard copy or as a PDF. You now have your first taste of what your book will look like when it is complete.

– – – – – –

What a thrill to see your book in page proofs, laid out just as it will appear in the final product. After all that work getting the text right during development and copyediting, the end must be in sight, right? It is! But first you must have those page proofs read by one more professional. Some publishing houses and many self-publishers are tempted to skip proofreading to save time and a little bit of money, but if it's up to you, don't cut corners. You may be surprised by what your proofreader uncovers!

AVOIDING THE POTHOLE
Get the Most out of Your Professional Design

A professional design is an essential part of offering your readers a high-quality book and a seamless reading experience, and it can be a powerful tool for selling books. The importance of a winning design is apparent in how consumers choose which books to read: good writing and editing may keep your readers turning the pages, but often it is the design that causes them to try your book in the first place.

As part of the design process, you will discuss your ideas with the designer or acquisitions editor, depending on your chosen route to publication. To help spur ideas on how best to infuse your book project with crisp design, review the competition. What do you like and dislike about the covers of books in your field or genre? Is there a cover you particularly want to emulate? Is there any part of the interior design that you would or would not want in your book? Try to review enough other books so that you can form an opinion about what works and what doesn't. Consider these questions when evaluating a design:

- Is the cover reflective of the contents of the book?

- Are the fonts appropriate for the genre or topic? For example, fonts used on science-fiction book covers are not the same as those used on self-help book covers.

- Does the tone of the book come through in the design of both the cover and the interior?

- Is the text easy to read?

- Do you like the design?

This may be a new skill for you, so immerse yourself until you feel comfortable explaining what you do and don't like. And have fun with it. This is your chance to be visually creative.

When you find designs you like, consider them as models for your own book. Your designer will want to hear your opinion before his or her work begins. Self-publishers, who control the design process, will have an easier time implementing their design ideas, whereas traditionally published authors have input but not final say. However, publishing houses also wish to offer a high-quality product, and the educated author can make valuable contributions to that conversation.

Often, the most effective interior and cover designs immerse your reader, from cover to cover, in the world that you have portrayed. *Derek Jeter: The Quiet Leader*, for example, might call on the Yankee pinstripes, "sporty" fonts, and baseball icons for design flare. For another example, *Growing and Cooking with Flax* might use illustrations of flax plants on the cover and chapter openers, with garden trowel icons placed with the gardening tips and wooden spoon icons with the cooking tips. In both instances, design elements from the cover are carried over to the interior so that the entire book has the same feel. Using design this way can be a powerful tool in delivering a pleasant reading experience for your audience.

Writers of a series can take this concept a step further. Design elements from the first book in a series may be used on the rest of the series. This is a great way to brand yourself and your series, an important feat of marketing. When you employ design this way, readers are able to pick your book out of a stack and know it is yours. Essentially, the marketing and promotion you have done for one book now apply to the other books in the series. Cover design elements may be used on your author website as well. These all contribute to the branding and packaging of your book and help raise your level of professionalism.

And now a word of caution: It's easy to go overboard with design, especially if you're a novice. Before selecting your five favorite fonts and a dozen theme-specific icons to sprinkle throughout your book, discuss your ideas with your designer or acquisitions editor. This type of cluttered design is the hallmark of an armchair designer and should be avoided. Ensure you are making full use of your packaging without overdoing it.

COVER COPY GUIDANCE

When it comes to selling your book, hand in hand with the cover design is the cover copy. What is cover copy? That is the marketing material that appears on the flaps of dust jackets and on the back covers of paperback books. It is also what usually appears in online bookstores under "Book Description."

Although there is a fairly simple formula for how to write cover copy, especially for nonfiction books (introductory paragraph, summary paragraph, bulleted list, and concluding paragraph), *good* cover copy can be hard to come by. Those working with a traditional publisher will have their cover copy arranged by the marketing department. Self-publishers will be well served to hire a copywriter or other marketing professional to write theirs for them. For those who decide to go it alone, keep these few pointers in mind:

◆ Aim for 250 words of back cover copy for a 6 × 9 paperback.

◆ If you are writing nonfiction, employ bulleted lists that tell readers "What's Inside."

◆ If you are writing fiction, make your synopsis a teaser, not a point-by-point plot outline.

◆ Include any endorsements you have received, but make sure they are concise (two or three sentences).

◆ Consider including an author photo and a brief, three- to four-sentence paragraph about your background that ties directly to the book.

◆ Write a snappy sales handle—around ten words that sum up the hook of your book—to be placed across the top of the back cover. (See Chapter 2 for more on this topic.)

Remember, this is sales copy and often the first thing your readers will read about your book. If it's boring, incomplete, or amateurish, potential readers will move on to the next book. If you're at all unsure of your abilities, hire a professional to help you. While it does cost money, the quality of your cover copy could make or break a sale.

Mapping Out Your Road to Success

Research the competition to understand the design conventions for your genre or field.

Form your own opinion about the interior and cover design you want for your book.

Supply your designer with a well-organized manuscript that is free of errors and that has any artwork keyed to the text.

Use design throughout your book to create a pleasant reading experience.

6

Fine-Tuning the Text
Proofreading, Author Review, and Final Revisions

ichard Curtis, a longtime literary agent now retired, once noted, "There's been a lot of talk lately about the decline of editing." That was twenty years ago, and you hear the same thing today. Why? Because publishers take shortcuts. With the advent of electronic editing, one area that some have deemed unnecessary is proofreading. You, however, are smart enough to know that in order to have a truly quality product that sells, you can't skip this step.

Proofreading can be the difference between a good review and a bad one. If you are self-publishing, it also saves you money, not to mention embarrassment, as you won't have to pay to fix errors discovered after the book is released. How can a proofreader make such an impact? Proofreaders serve as a safeguard against anything the copyeditor may have missed and any errors that may have been introduced between the copyediting stage and page layout.

Traditionally published authors will not work directly with the proofreader but will be tasked with reviewing the proofs themselves (the subject of this chapter's Pothole). Further, the in-house production editor may relay to the author any questions or concerns

Everyone needs an editor, even copyeditors. For the highest-quality book, use a proofreader and perform your own thorough check of the page proofs as well.

that the proofreader has raised and will enlist the author's help in resolving these problems.

Self-publishers, as always, are in the driver's seat and will be directly involved in hiring the proofreader, reviewing the proof-reader's changes, relaying those changes to the designer, and check-ing the revised pages to ensure all changes were made correctly. You can expect to go through second and third rounds of revisions until the pages are as clean as possible and ready for publication.

Proofreading generally takes about two to three weeks, unless your book is quite long. As the author, you will have this time to perform your own simultaneous review of the pages. Those who will be hiring a freelance proofreader can expect to pay between $12 and $25 an hour. Self-publishers who will be checking the proofreader's work should allow themselves an additional week to perform this task. Receiving revised pages from the designer may take another two to four weeks, depending on length and com-plexity of the book, the number of changes to be made, and the designer's schedule.

WHAT YOU CAN EXPECT FROM YOUR PROOFREADER

Proofreaders are often also copyeditors by trade, and in fact they look for many of the same errors the copyeditor was supposed to fix, with a few exceptions. Grammar, punctuation, style, consistency, and sense remain essential. Questions of word choice and flow take a backseat, however, and will be fixed as time and money allow. (See the Pothole "Revise Your Manuscript One Last time" in Chapter 4 for an in-depth discussion of the different types of errors.)

Art-heavy books, books with many cross-references, and books that have a hefty set of endnotes benefit greatly from proofreading. Photos and their corresponding captions have a way of becom-ing mismatched. A proofreader will spot this error as well as any instances of a photo or illustration being inserted in the wrong place. Cross-references also are liable to be incorrect in page proofs, as you may have moved chunks of text without updating the cross-references, and endnotes are notoriously difficult for all involved to keep track of. Because the proofreader has a cleaner text to work with than the copyeditor did, he or she is less distracted by big or messy changes and can double-check that all of these elements are coming together properly. The proofreader will also mark any errors of page layout, such as very tight or very loose lines, a page with fewer than four lines, or a missing or misspelled running head.

Your proofreader may also raise concerns that were not satisfied during copyediting. Sometimes these are issues that have been discussed and dealt with; other times they are new concerns that require some attention. Exactly how these queries are handled will depend on which publishing route you have chosen, how big of a problem was uncovered, and how much effort will be required to correct or adjust the text to resolve the problem. For example, if a proofreader notes that a passage in chapter 9 of your book repeats verbatim from chapter 6, that will likely need to be fixed regardless of the consequences. If the proofreader notes that you have used the word *outraged* three times in two paragraphs, that might not be fixed. In traditional publishing, it is up to the in-house production editor to make that call; self-publishers have to use their own judgment based on time and money allowed.

When it comes to the text corrections, you may wonder how these errors made it all the way into page proofs if this is what the copyeditor was hired to fix. One common reason for errors appearing in page proofs is that the manuscript required a heavy copyedit. When a copyeditor has to spend a lot of time on big-picture issues such as adding transitions, moving paragraphs, or rewriting convoluted sentences, his or her focus may be taken away from the finer points. Comma errors, dangling modifiers, and inconsistent spelling can be overlooked. The proofreader is essential in these circumstances, as he or she will be able to uncover these smaller errors now that the big picture is in place. Note that this is one way manuscript development can save you time and money; such errors are less likely to appear in page proofs if the manuscript has gone through development and the copyeditor is able to focus on punctuation and grammar instead of organization.

So, what if the CE made very few changes to the book? Do you still need a proofreader? The answer is yes, for two reasons.

First, changes are often made between copyediting and layout, and errors may have been introduced at that time. Second, and just as important, different editors have different strengths. Your CE may have forgotten a grammar or style point that the proofreader remembers—and fixes. Even editors need editors, and that is why it is so essential that a proofreader be used. Thoroughly revising your manuscript before copyediting, as well as using a qualified, professional copyeditor, are two steps that you can take to reduce the number of changes made during proofreading.

WHAT YOUR PROOFREADER EXPECTS FROM YOU

Proofreaders, even those working with self-publishers, tend to have little interaction with authors. They do their work, return the pages to the publishing house or author, and say, "Call me if you have questions." Traditionally published authors will likely never speak to their proofreader. Self-publishers will have hired

Will You Have an Index?

With creative nonfiction being a notable exception, most nonfiction books do well to have an index. Traditional publishers will decide if your book needs an index, and, if it does, the publisher may pay for the expense or your contract may state that the cost of hiring a professional indexer will be deducted from your royalties. For self-publishers, if you want an index for your book, you can either compile it yourself or hire a professional indexer. Of the ten or so indexes I have seen that were prepared by the author, only one was close to professional quality. It takes a particular mind to do an index well. If you don't have a natural affinity for this kind of work, hire someone who does. The cost of an index varies based on the density of the text, but you can plan between $3 and $6 a book page for indexing. The index should be created from the *revised* page proofs, not the manuscript or first page proofs. The reason is that material may be moved or deleted at manuscript stage, and changes during the first round of page proofs can cause material to move from one page to another (called reflow).

the proofreader themselves and may follow up with questions after reviewing the editing.

If you are working directly with the proofreader, you can ensure a good relationship by being timely and polite. Open communication is also key. Alert your proofreader to any issues that came up at copyediting that you already know you do not want to change or, conversely, decisions that were made after copyediting that will need to be implemented now. The proofreader is usually the last professional to read the book from beginning to end, and he or she is in the best position to ensure consistency on these last-minute changes.

When you review the proofreading, if you have questions, compile them and either e-mail them to your proofreader or arrange a phone consult. By now you will be familiar with the sting of editing and hopefully will remember to not take it personally or get angry at your proofreader. Self-publishers, you are free to make or not make any suggested changes, so ultimately the decision will be yours if you do not like the proofreading. But once again, remember that you have hired a professional for a reason: this person is an expert in the field. Your concerns may be the result of bad proofreading, in which case you have the right to be upset and may need to undo some of your proofreader's work. Also consider, however, that your proofreader may have reasons for his or her changes that you are not aware of. Discuss these issues with your proofreader before making your final judgment.

ROADSIDE ASSISTANT

Blythe Hurley
Former proofreader and copyeditor

Blythe Hurley is the former owner of Blythe Hurley Editorial Services in Chicago and now works as a project editor for a research and professional services firm in the human capital sector. She is the former managing editor of a major sports book publisher and worked as a full-time freelance editorial services provider from 2006 to 2013.

Why do you feel proofreading is so important?
First I would say that to an educated audience, finding typos or other mistakes in a book makes one doubt the professionalism and quality of both the author and his or her product. Second, while authors may be experts regarding the subject matter about which they write, they are more than likely not experts regarding grammar, syntax, or the publishing process. Why *wouldn't* you want an expert to help make your book—something into which you have put so much hard work and passion—as good as it can be?

Many authors question the need for having both a proofreader and a copyeditor. With more than twenty years in the publishing industry, I can tell you from experience that many strange things can and do happen when a book goes through the layout and design process. I have seen designers edit copy in books without ever alerting the author or editor as to the changes being made. I have seen words, lines, paragraphs, images, and even whole chapters inadvertently dropped or rearranged. I have seen text or artwork from something else a designer is working on accidentally pasted into a layout. Everyone makes mistakes, and it's your proofreader's job to go over your book with a fine-toothed comb to make sure nothing like that has happened with your project.

Last, I would say that many people do not realize that the point of having their work edited and proofread is not only to correct grammar or spelling; it's also to have someone read the book from a fresh perspective with no emotional attachment to the material. Oftentimes, authors spend so much time on and put so much passion into their work that they become overly attached to their own prose. Since the proofreader works on the book after it has been designed, he or she is the first real audience for the project as it will actually look to potential customers. You are paying them for their expertise and experience to make sure your product is in keeping with what they know about the publishing marketplace.

What advice do you have for new authors working with a proofreader?
If your proofreader or editor tells you something isn't working, do your very best to put aside any defensiveness and consider any

suggestions he or she makes. Even the most gifted of writers can use a fresh pair of eyes to review their work.

Also, be sure to communicate clearly with proofreaders about any special concerns you have, particular issues for which you would like them to look, or facets of the project of which they should be aware. Is there something that you changed during editing that you want double-checked? Is there some special formatting or word choice you've used that you don't want them to change? Are you still trying to make sure that you've been consistent with issues? These are all things that the proofreader can certainly help with.

THE PROCESS

Traditionally published authors will be only minimally involved in the proofreading process. Self-published authors will have more involvement, but because proofreading tends to mean much fewer changes than copyediting, their task of reviewing the editing is getting easier and easier. Both types of authors will review page proofs for themselves as well and make refinements. The designer will then input all changes, provide revised proofs, and then make any additional changes until the pages are as clean as possible.

Traditional Publishing

Proofreading begins when the in-house production editor (PE) sends either a hard copy or a PDF of the page proofs to the proofreader, keeping a copy for herself to review. Simultaneously, copies will be sent to the author (that's you!), the in-house design specialist (if applicable), the acquisitions editor, and possibly the marketing department. In much the same way the design sample was handled, each of these individuals will be looking at different aspects. All parties, including the proofreader, will mark their changes and return the pages to the PE on a set schedule, usually in two to three weeks. The PE then compiles the changes onto a master document. In the process, she determines if some changes should not be made and, if there are any conflicts, which changes supersede the others. You may receive a call regarding queries from the proofreader or contradictory directives. A common instance of a contradictory directive occurs when there are multiple authors. Ideally the lead

Coeditions: E-Books and Printed Books

Creating an e-book has become so easy that many authors are tempted to jump right in before completing the editing process. In fact, some traditional publishers do the same thing; although the printed book receives a proofread, the e-book may not. If it is up to you, do not succumb to this temptation.

In my work with one self-publishing author recently, we were discussing the publication date for his book and just how long it would be before he had a bound book ready to sell. It looked like he might not have his books in time for the start of his ideal selling period. Anxious to get his book on the market, this author had an idea. Why not put the e-book out right now, even before the copyediting was complete, since that takes very little time, and then continue with the editing for the printed book! Here is why not: You have only one chance to make a first impression. If you put out a book that still has a lot of errors in it, you have burned bridges with all the people who bought the inferior product. These first customers are likely to be the people most interested in your book, and their good reading experience is critical in getting more people to buy your book. Self-publishers in particular cannot afford to risk their reputations this way. For years I didn't believe that bad editing would sink a book (this from a committed and passionate editor), but with the advent of reader reviews on Amazon and other online sites, I have learned that lesson. And once those bad reviews are up, they don't come down and you have to work twice as hard to get your reputation back.

Traditionally published authors may be able to negotiate this point in their contracts, ensuring that the e-book will be created from the final, proofread file. For self-publishers, the decision is theirs to make. Whatever path you choose, don't waste your money and all your hard work by taking shortcuts and releasing a book tarnished by errors. Insist on a final proofread to ensure the highest-quality, most marketable book possible.

author will have resolved these conflicts, but if that hasn't happened, the PE will manage them.

Once all changes have been compiled and all queries have been answered, the pages are sent back to the designer so that the requested changes can be made. The designer then supplies the production editor with revised pages. The PE checks the revised pages against the master document to ensure all changes were made correctly and performs some final checks to verify that no more changes are required. Often, more changes *are* required—the table of contents is notorious for requiring last-minute changes— and revisions are sent back and forth another one or two times until the pages are as clean as they can be. At that point the project is in its final stage before becoming a real live book.

Self-Publishing

The proofreading process in self-publishing begins with the author. First you must find and hire a proofreader. (See the sidebar "5 Steps to Hiring a Freelance Editor" in Chapter 3 for guidance.) When you arrange the proofreading, set out a schedule and determine whether you will send your proofreader a hard copy of the page proofs or a PDF. If you decide to send a PDF, you must then decide if you want the proofreader to print out the pages and work on hard copy or work directly in the PDF file using the Sticky Notes function. There are pros and cons to each method. Before you make your final decision, however, coordinate with your designer to find out how he or she would prefer to receive changes.

For the proofreader, it is often easier and faster to work on hard copy because corrections can be made directly on the page instead of having to indicate with words exactly where the changes belong, as is the case with PDFs. Faster and easier tends to mean less expensive. For you as the author, having the proofreader work on hard copy means learning proofreaders' marks so that you can understand the changes he is suggesting. These marks are not difficult to understand, and you can easily look them up in *Merriam-Webster's* under "proofreaders' marks," but it is an extra hurdle.

With Sticky Notes in the PDF, although time-consuming and at times frustrating for the proofreader, you as author are able to simply read the notes to find out what changes the proofreader is suggesting, and you can easily delete those changes that you opt not to make before passing the file on to the designer. Working this way offers a savings on postage as well as shipping time. However, you need to be familiar enough with Acrobat Reader, a generally straightforward program to use, to navigate the Sticky Notes. As indicated above, you may pay a little extra in proofreading charges given the added time it takes the proofreader to complete the editing, but you may decide that the convenience and savings on shipping are worth it. There is no right answer; it is a matter of preference.

When your proofreader has completed the editing, he will return the page proofs to you so that you can review his work. You may find a handful of queries from the proofreader, but if the copyediting was thorough, these shouldn't be too grievous. You will look over the proofreader's edits, determine which ones you want to keep, cross out or delete the ones you don't want to make, and then send the edited proofs to the designer to have the changes implemented. If you have questions about the editing, compile them and call or e-mail your proofreader for clarification. Most proofreaders are more than happy to explain why they did what they did, and you want to avoid undoing the proofreader's work and introducing problems. Inconsistencies often arise when authors add material or revert to an older version at this point in the production process.

Save Money. Hire a Proofreader.

Although it may be counterintuitive to say that paying for a proofreader saves you money, remember that at this point your designer is the one implementing changes, and his or her time can be pricey. Getting all of your final changes in at one time will minimize the time your designer needs to spend fixing your book. Also, if you skip proofreading and then have to make changes after the book publishes, not only will you have to pay the designer to make the changes, but you will also have to reprint your book and/or upload a new version of the e-book, which can also cost money.

From here you will work directly with your designer to ensure that all changes are made. You may opt to perform a complete second proofreading of your own or you may do as a traditional publisher does and simply verify that the requested changes were made, double-check the table of contents and running heads, and review the pages for obvious errors. Even this limited review will usually turn up a few more corrections. When you are satisfied that the text is as clean as you can get it, or when time runs out, you are ready to make your book a reality.

- - - - - -

Inside Tip

If you are working on hard copy, it is best *not* to erase the proofreader's changes, as you may want to look back at the proofreader's work sometime in the future. Instead, simply cross out any suggested changes you don't want to keep and write "stet." Similarly, if you are working electronically, save the file with a new name before deleting unwanted changes.

Proofreading is your last line of defense against errors before you launch your book. Take care to catch as many mistakes now as you can. If you are being traditionally published, several other people will also be reviewing the proofs, but that doesn't mean you won't catch something others have missed. If you are self-publishing, you hold the reins. Polish your book now before it launches. You can save yourself time, money, and embarrassment by catching errors before publication.

If you have been working continuously from manuscript development, it has been about six months or so since you started down the road to publication. You have seen your manuscript transform from the original "final" draft that you submitted to your agent, acquisitions editor, developmental editor, or copyeditor into something quite different. You have a pretty good idea of what your final product will look like, since you have seen both the interior (page proofs) and the final cover. Now you are about to realize your goal of a high-quality, highly marketable book, whether that means printing and binding it or converting it into an e-book.

AVOIDING THE POTHOLE
Know What to Look for When Reviewing Page Proofs

A common stumbling block for new authors is what to do with page proofs when they receive them from their designer. This is especially true of self-publishers, who lack the helping hand of an in-house editor to guide them. While the proofreader is hard at work polishing the text, you will also have a copy of the page proofs to review. If you make good use of this opportunity, you can help ensure that your book is of the highest quality.

By this point in the production process, making changes has become expensive, and traditional publishing houses will often limit the number of changes an author can make. Self-publishers will quickly find out why. Some designers charge *per change* after the manuscript has been laid out. It is also time-consuming, as one significant change could mean that an entire page or several pages need to be remade. Such issues arise more often in nonfiction books, but fiction authors should also keep these points in mind. Indeed, some contracts specify that an author will be responsible for the cost of changes at page proofs if they go beyond a certain level.

About this time, you may begin to hear the phrase "true errors." These are the types of errors that are indisputable: spelling errors, grammar errors, and the like. They are errors that could be embarrassing or trigger bad reviews if they made it into the final book. Other changes that you may consider errors are not what would normally be called true errors—for example, using the same adjective two sentences in a row or using a semicolon when you would rather use a period and start a new sentence. Self-publishers are not restricted by this definition of a true error when marking their changes, but authors working with a traditional publisher very well may be. This is another reason why it is so important to be thorough at the copyediting and query resolution stage. Word choice, transitions, and other finessing are best done early.

When you receive your copy of the page proofs, besides reading the text, you may also wish to look at other aspects of the proofs. This is particularly important for self-publishers, who do not have an in-house editor to ensure the quality of layout and design. The following are some basic checks that you can perform:

♦ Check that all pages have been included.

♦ Check the running heads. Common problems include a missing running head, misspellings, and a running head that does not match the chapter in which it appears. For fiction and creative nonfiction books, running heads are usually author name on the left page and book title on the right page. For other nonfiction books, it's usually book title on the left and chapter title on the right, or part title on the left and chapter title on the right. There should never be a running head on a blank page or chapter opener.

♦ Ensure that design elements are treated consistently. That means that level 1 heads all look the same, level 2 heads all look the same, and so on. Authors with a copy of the design sample can compare the proofs to the sample.

♦ Check the table of contents against the text. Make sure page numbers are correct and that chapter titles match the text. Page numbers on chapter openers usually appear at the bottom of the page.

♦ Check that artwork is placed correctly and that captions match the image.

♦ Check for odd characters in tables and graphs.

♦ Check that facing pages "twin"—that is, align top and bottom.

Your proofreader is also looking for these errors, but don't assume that he or she will catch everything. You have the opportunity now to make these corrections. And yes, these fall into the category of "true errors" along with spelling and grammatical errors.

Getting these details right can have a huge impact on whether your book looks professionally made or hastily thrown together. Those using assisted self-publishing in particular, where quality is hit or miss, will find that knowing what to look for in page proofs makes a big difference in their end product.

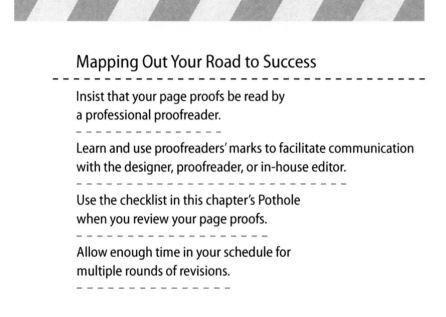

Mapping Out Your Road to Success

Insist that your page proofs be read by a professional proofreader.

Learn and use proofreaders' marks to facilitate communication with the designer, proofreader, or in-house editor.

Use the checklist in this chapter's Pothole when you review your page proofs.

Allow enough time in your schedule for multiple rounds of revisions.

7

Making It Real
Printers, Distributors, and E-Book Companies

Ahh, the last piece of the puzzle. After all your hard work, you are now ready to make your book a reality. Whether that is as a print book, an e-book, or both, your manuscript will continue its transformation at the hands of printers and binders and e-book companies. While traditional publishing houses take care of these tasks behind the scenes, self-publishers are deeply involved. This chapter explains what each of these vendors does, what distribution options are available, and what they mean for you. These last steps are crucial to producing a professional-looking product that can stand up to the competition. In the Pothole at the end of the chapter we look at what goes on the copyright page and where that information comes from. Again, the appearance of professionalism is at the heart of this section.

The final step in publishing a book is actually several small steps. Self-publishers will do well to read the fine print before making any decisions. Traditionally published authors can sit back and enjoy the ride.

PRINTING AND BINDING OPTIONS

If you plan to have a printed book, you have some decisions to make. Do you use a digital printer or an offset printer? Do you contract with a printer and then keep an inventory, or do you use a distributor? What about print-on-demand? Each decision has its upsides and downsides. Let's look at them in turn.

Digital vs. Offset Printing

First, let's define our terms. A digital printer uses what is essentially a very large Xerox machine to print books on various sizes of paper. These pages are then hot-glued into a cover. (This is what is meant by "perfect binding," a term you will likely encounter when exploring printing options.) An offset printer uses a large printing press that requires very large paper and then folds it into groups, called signatures. The signatures are then trimmed and either hot-glued or sewn into the binding.

In years past, the clear winner on quality was offset printing. Unfortunately, offset printing requires so much setup that for it to be cost-effective, you have to print at least a thousand copies to reach any kind of economy of scale. Yet, digital printing, a much cheaper solution, was of such inferior quality that looking at the print quality alone was a fast way to tell if a book had been self-published, and *self-published* translated to "not worth the time." Luckily for self-publishers, times have changed and digital printing has made great strides in quality. It does not quite match that of offset printing—particularly in the area of binding—but it has become a viable option for those who plan to print fewer than a thousand copies, and it still looks professional enough to compete in the marketplace. For print runs higher than a thousand copies, offset printing remains the first choice for most authors and for traditional publishers.

So what does your printer expect from you? Working with a printer, whether offset or digital, requires many of the same skills as when working with other vendors: you need to be respectful and communicate well. It is best to contact printers at the design stage, when you will discuss trim size, printing and binding materials, and the print specifications. According to Davis Scott, a veteran of the printing industry, "Decisions made without printer input may result in extra expense and/or an end result that is not to the author's expectations." Working with a professional designer who can submit files to the printer in the best possible shape also makes a big difference in the final product. "It is very important that the designer knows what works best in the pressroom," Davis notes. "What may look good on a computer screen may not be possible to re-create in the final product. Or the printer may be able to offer a more efficient process to achieve the same result." As is so often the case, you'll want to maintain an open line of communication between you and the printer so that everyone's expectations are met.

About two to four weeks after the designer sends final files to the printer, you will receive a printer proof. This is the very, very last chance you have to review the book before it is printed and bound. The proof may come to you as a mock-up of the book, with pages cut and glued into the cover, or you may receive the cover and interior separately. Review these proofs with a fine-toothed comb. It is very expensive to make changes at this point, but if some egregious error has somehow slipped past the publishing team, you must fix it now or wait until the book's next printing (i.e., reprint).

ROADSIDE ASSISTANT
Davis Scott
Former printing and binding professional

Davis Scott, now retired, spent forty-four years in the printing business, including twenty-nine years in book printing sales. He has worked with publishers of all sizes and has been involved in the production of more than ten thousand new titles and fifteen thousand reprints.

What do you expect from an author in the way of a good working relationship?
A good working relationship begins with an agreement on expectations—what the parties expect from one another. When this groundwork is not laid out in advance, in some detail, misunderstandings can arise later, complicating the successful completion of the contract.

What are some of the common mistakes you've seen?

In my twenty-nine years of book printing sales, and hundreds of contacts with new authors, the most frequent mistake is their wanting to go to press without a clear understanding of the business of publishing. Whenever they ask how many books they should print, my response is always, how many books can they sell? Do they have a business plan? How much research have they done on competing books? What place do they expect their book to hold in the market? What channels of distribution are they going to use? Have they thought about working capital? Suppliers want to be paid well before any revenues start to come in. Do they understand that books shipped do not necessarily equal books sold? How are they going to price their book, both in print and e-book formats? Should they consider producing a small number of digital copies for review and feedback before pursuing a larger offset run? These are all critically important issues, and after seeing too many books fail, I learned to coach new customers that these items must all be addressed before giving any printer a purchase order.

Further down the process are editing and design. Too often, the new author/self-publisher will try to cut corners in these areas, either by using a friend or relative having no specific book experience or, worse, by trying to do it themselves. An English teacher is not necessarily an editor, and someone in commercial design may not have the skill set to produce an effective cover or text layout. Appearances and effective editing, or lack thereof, can make or break a sale.

How willing are they to go out and promote their book, both pre- and post-publishing? Do they have a social networking presence? Do they speak to groups, and will the book lend itself to back-of-the-room sales? Do they know how to get and execute effective media opportunities? Barring exceptional luck, a poorly promoted book has little chance for success. Selling an e-book only does take away the issue of up-front printing costs, but all the other factors remain.

Can you share a best or worst author experience?

My best experiences were those where the author/publisher understood and executed all of the items discussed here. My biggest disappointments were those who otherwise produced a good book but failed to market it effectively. It is much, much more effective to find and reach out to an audience than it is to hope an audience will find you.

What advice do you have for new authors?

Accept that you don't know all the answers, and seek help from professionals and publishers' groups. Don't overreach in what you are trying to accomplish.

Print-on-Demand (POD)

First, a word of caution. As was the case with assisted self-publishing, print-on-demand (POD) companies have a pretty bad reputation. Not all of it is warranted; however, because the good guys and the bad guys both call themselves print-on-demand, you have to do your homework before signing any contracts. Ask around and read reviews online. Then choose a company with a good reputation for quality and customer service.

Print-on-demand is a relatively new option for authors. As the name implies, books printed this way are printed in very small quantities, often less than five hundred copies and sometimes as they are purchased. It's similar to a made-to-order hamburger: (1) the buyer places an order, (2) the printer prints and binds only the number of books in the order, and (3) the printer then ships the order to the consumer in as little as twenty-four hours. This is accomplished via digital printing, and quality varies based on the POD vendor. The main benefit to this setup is that the author does not have to hold any inventory. The per-unit price is higher than if you were printing five hundred or more copies at once, but there is no cost for storage or time commitment for filling orders. One of the biggest downsides, assuming the quality meets your standards and the unit price is manageable, is that bookstores don't like to carry print-on-demand books due to their

Inside Tip

Not all bookstores will work with all print-on-demand companies, even when distribution is included. Consider contacting any bookstores you hope will carry your book to find out their policies before selecting your POD printer.

distribution setup. The reasons for this are explained more fully in the following section.

Other drawbacks to print-on-demand are a loss of creative control, in that you may have to select template interior and cover designs for your book in lieu of working with a professional designer, and you often have a limited number of trim sizes to choose from. In addition, with some services, the POD company holds the ISBN. That means the company is technically the pub-

Knowing a Scam When You See One

"There are a lot of people out there who will gladly take your money and give you nothing in return."

"Really?"

This is an actual exchange I had with a new author who was getting ready to purchase a publishing package from a large publishing services company known by many to be disreputable. The company was having a sale, and the representative told this man that he had to act now because "the sale ends today." The author had no idea what was included in the package and didn't even know what questions to ask, but the high-pressure tactics were working. He didn't want to miss out on a great price and the opportunity to see his book in print *right now*. He called me for guidance.

After gathering as many details as I could, I explained that what this company was offering wasn't worth even the reduced price—there were no editing or design considerations, no quality assurance—and he didn't need to rush into a decision as important as which company to use to help him publish his book. Luckily, I was able to talk him out of the deal, telling him to wait until he was ready before making a decision. It saved him several hundred dollars and, more important, a huge headache when he realized exactly what he was *not* getting in the deal.

It is important to keep your head when dealing with unknown vendors. Be your own advocate. Ask questions, and if the answers are murky or if you feel pressured to make a decision, get off the phone or walk away from the computer. Even a few hundred dollars is too much to spend when you don't know what you're paying for.

lisher, not you, which may have legal implications for you if you intend to set up a publishing company.

Some of the popular and well-respected print-on-demand companies include CreateSpace (a branch of Amazon.com), Lightning Source (a branch of Ingram), and Lulu. POD companies have widely varying price structures and package options, so you will need to read very carefully about the companies you are considering. Moreover, some POD companies have bad reputations for scamming authors or providing lower quality than promised. The confusion is compounded because one company may own a number of other companies. For example, Author Solutions, which has a bad reputation among many self-publishers, owns AuthorHouse, DellArte, iUniverse, Trafford Publishing, West Bow, and Xlibris. Penguin Group just purchased the parent company, but it is unclear if this will improve the current standards at Author Solutions.

When researching POD vendors, be particularly wary of the marketing packages that they offer, as they often promise more than they can deliver and the packages cost significantly more than they are worth. The Science Fiction and Fantasy Writers of America website (www.sfwa.org) has an excellent discussion on POD, complete with pros, cons, and red flags. Preditors and Editors (www.pred-ed.com) is another good resource for information on a variety of publishing vendors, including POD services, and their reputations. Educate yourself before signing up with any one company.

DISTRIBUTION AND ORDER FULFILLMENT

If you are a self-publisher with printed books, you have to figure out a way to get your books in front of your readers. The most obvious places you can do that are bookstores, conventions, talks, online bookstores, or your website. In addition, you need an inventory and order fulfillment solution, whether that means using a distributor or wholesaler or doing it yourself. What is right for you depends on where you plan to sell your books, how they will be printed, and how many you plan to print.

Working with a Distributor or Wholesaler

Wholesalers and distributors have much in common, but there are a few key differences. Most important, distribution companies have a sales force that sells your book to bookstores, while wholesalers do not. For this reason, distributors tend to be more discerning about whom they work with, and often they are not interested in establishing an account with a publisher unless he or she has multiple titles. Some very large wholesalers also discriminate against self-publishers, while smaller wholesale companies are more likely to work with an independent or one-title publisher.

Still, if you meet the qualifications, there is a lot to be said for working with a distributor. These vendors have standing relationships with bookstores and are in a much better position to get your book on the shelves and in front of readers than you are as an individual. If you are planning to have a significant number of books printed and you want your book to be carried in bookstores, you should seriously consider finding a distributor, either on your own or through your printer.

Before you sign a contract, however, the distributor must approve your book. Because distributors make money based on how many books they sell for you, they have to believe that your book is marketable. Many smaller distributors specialize in a few genres, while larger distributors may work in all fields. But as Jacqueline Simonds states in her article for the Association of Publishers for Special Sales, "Bigger is not necessarily better. Smaller doesn't necessarily mean friendlier." In fact, the largest distributors, Ingram and Baker & Taylor, do not work with independent publishers unless they have at least ten titles to sell. Ingram has a separate arm, called IngramSpark, that works with micropublish-

Inside Tip

How many books should you print? Refer to your book business plan to figure (1) how many copies you need to sell to break even, and (2) how many copies you think you can sell. When you crunch the numbers, account for storage costs, if applicable, as well as any price break you receive for printing more copies. Then aim low. Remember that you can always print more. Once the books are printed, however, you have to pay for them whether you sell them or not.

ers. In July 2013 Baker & Taylor purchased Bookmasters to finally enter the print-on-demand arena.

Once you're accepted by the distributor, you sign a contract in which you agree to sell your books to the distributor for between 55 percent and 68 percent off the list price. (If you sell directly to a bookstore you give *the bookstore* the 55 percent discount.) That means if *Derek Jeter: The Quiet Leader* is priced at $10, the distribution company pays you between $3.20 and $4.50 per book sold, the bookstore takes its share, and the distributor keeps the rest. This can be a bit of a surprise to the uninitiated; you must take this discount under consideration when you set your cover price. Further, if the distributor fails to sell your books to bookstores, it is able to return the books to you. And, distributors are not marketers. They have a sales force that works to get your book on bookstores' shelves. Promotion—letting readers know that the book is available and where to find it—is up to you. These are the downsides.

The upsides are that you (1) don't have to hold inventory in your garage or pay for storage, (2) don't have to package and ship books, and (3) are able to get your book onto shelves in stores that you would not be able to reach on your own. Distributors do all this for you, and then send you a check. That leaves you with more time to work on other aspects of the publishing business, like marketing and writing more books.

If a distributor is not an option for you, a wholesaler may be. Wholesalers will take care of inventory, ship your books, and make your book available to bookstores. They do not sell the book, but they do act as a professional point person for bookstores to interface with.

While the list of upsides may seem short, if you plan to sell your book through bookstores, using either a distributor or a wholesaler may be the way to go.

DIY Inventory and Order Fulfillment

So, who *doesn't* need a distributor? Print-on-demand companies generally have built-in distribution options, so you would not need to find a distributor or wholesaler on your own (although they still can't reach many brick-and-mortar stores). In addition, if you are planning to sell your book mainly through your website, through local outlets where you have connections, or via speaking engagements, conferences, and the like—and you aren't concerned with being on bookstore shelves—then you don't need a distributor. Authors in this situation generally keep a supply of books at their home or in a storage unit, manage the inventory themselves, and package and ship purchased books as they are ordered. Other books may be sold at signings or at the back of the room of a conference or talk. Those who are printing only a small number of books may find this a good option, as their inventory will be more manageable and storage costs will be limited. Be sure to consider the cost of postage and the time involved in packing and shipping books when deciding if this is the right path for you.

SELECTING AN E-BOOK COMPANY

Today it is easier than ever to create an e-book. All you have to do is upload your file to an e-book company's website, let some magical conversion take place, and, voilà, you have an e-book. With the help of *Perfect Bound*, however, you know that making a *quality* e-book takes more than just uploading the first draft of your manuscript to the first website you come across. In this section we explore the various companies that can help you do it right as well as some of the common mistakes to avoid to make sure you aren't wasting your time or ruining your reputation in the e-book publication process.

The Big Names in the Field

BookBaby, Smashwords, Nook Press, Kobo, Kindle Direct Publishing (KDP). You'll find numerous e-book companies available to you, but these are some of the biggest and most respected. They can be broken into two groups: BookBaby, Smashwords, and Kobo are full-service e-book companies that convert and

A Word on File Formats for E-Books

Amazon's Kindle does not run the same type of file that other e-readers do. Whereas Barnes & Noble's Nook, Apple's iPad and iPhone, Kobo, and most other e-readers accept ePub files, the Kindle requires either an AZW or a MOBI file. If you wish to have your book available to read on more than just a Kindle, you will need to convert your manuscript file more than once or find a company that will do so for you.

distribute your e-book; Nook Press and KDP are places that convert and distribute your e-book specifically for their platforms. The following is a summary of what each of these companies offers and how they make their money.

BookBaby

BookBaby (www.bookbaby.com) offers three tiers of pricing for authors, from free to $249 as of 2014. The free package does not offer conversion, and BookBaby takes 15 percent of net sales. Customer service is limited to e-mail, and no proof of the book is available. All of that means you have to be confident your file is in tip-top shape before choosing this package. The standard and premium packages, however, offer valuable additional services. These include file conversion to ePub or MOBI, a quality check on e-readers, proofs for the author, and free conversion of a limited number of graphics. BookBaby will accept your manuscript in Microsoft Word, PDF, InDesign, and several other file formats, which some companies don't do. All packages come with Book-Promo, a marketing benefit that includes free book reviews and promotion with some key players as well as valuable discounts.

As far as which package to choose, it is almost certainly worth paying extra to be able to review proofs, not only because you want to ensure that you are putting out the best possible product, but also because the company charges extra if you want to make changes after the e-book has published; not all companies charge you to make changes. Between the standard and the premium packages, the big difference is that with the standard package, BookBaby again takes 15 percent of net sales. With the premium package, you keep 100 percent of sales. Outside of the packages, you can also purchase cover design, print-on-demand services, and ISBNs.

Smashwords

A recognized leader in e-books, Smashwords (www.smashwords .com) offers e-book conversion as well as distribution to all of the major retailers. There is no charge to set up an account, but Smashwords does take a 15 percent cut of net sales through its store and 40 percent for sales through other retailers. To have your file converted, you need to supply a Word file; no other file formats are accepted. Also, the demands for formatting that Word file can be a bit persnickety. However, Smashwords is able to convert your manuscript to multiple formats, and the company is known for having excellent author resources to help you ensure that your book publishes as expected. The website has numerous free booklets and videos to teach you how to make and sell your book. In that same vein, all changes and updates to your file are free—a potentially huge benefit. Smashwords doesn't offer any other services, but that also means it won't try to sell you anything beyond e-book conversion and distribution.

Kindle Direct Publishing (KDP)

As a division of Amazon, KDP (https://kdp.amazon.com) is huge. There is no charge for setting up an account. Instead, Amazon takes 30 percent of the list price for each book you sell, while you keep the other 70 percent, with two main caveats:

1. Books must be sold within Amazon's stipulated list of countries (a short list but one that hits the hot spots). Outside of these territories and the company's cut jumps to 65 percent.

2. To qualify for the 70/30 split, books must be priced between $2.99 and $9.99. Above or below that and the split changes dramatically, with Amazon again taking 65 percent.

KDP accepts several different formats for conversion, including Microsoft Word, PDF, and ePub, but MS Word remains the pre-

> **What About Apple?**
> Right now you may be wondering where iBooks fits into this scheme. A free app from Apple, iBooks Author offers limited creation and publishing capabilities exclusively for iPads and Macs. More functionality is likely coming. Keep your eyes peeled.

ferred format. KDP does not offer conversion to other e-book formats and is only available on Kindles and Kindle-enabled devices. One notable benefit to KDP is that you can upload a corrected file for free. If changes are significant, you can have KDP contact people who already bought the book to let them know a revised edition is ready. You may also want to look into the KDP Select program, which allows you to offer your book for free for promotions and to reach Amazon Prime customers. To take part in this package, you must agree to sell your book only through Amazon for the entire promotional period. That is a drawback, but with Amazon being as large as it is, many self-published authors give it a try.

For a long time one of the biggest downsides to working with KDP was the difficulty of navigating its website. The website has been significantly improved in recent months, but pertinent information is not always where you would expect it to be. Creating your e-book is easy, but the finances are complicated and getting answers to your questions is hard. Be sure to read *everything*.

Nook Press

Barnes & Noble also has an e-book service, called Nook Press (www.nookpress.com). As with KDP, account setup is free, and the pricing structure is very similar: For books priced between $2.99 and $9.99, authors receive 65 percent of royalties. Above or below that range and the author gets 40 percent. Books are available for purchase through the Nook Bookstore and devices running Nook software.

To ensure your manuscript appears as desired when converted into an e-book, Nook Press has a tool called Manuscript Editor. Once you upload your manuscript to Manuscript Editor, you can make adjustments to the text and layout and then preview the final file as it will appear on a Nook. (You can actually create your entire manuscript in Manuscript Editor if you have the inclination.) You are able to edit or replace your manuscript for free at any time. The site also provides helpful, easy-to-follow instructions on how to format your manuscript before uploading it, to reduce the chance of errors in your e-book.

Kobo

For international sales, Kobo (www.kobo.com) is at the forefront. This company offers two paths to e-book publication, one with file conversion (called Kobo Writing Life) and one without (Kobo Publisher Operations). Writing Life is designed for small publishers and authors and is the path you would likely choose as a self-publisher. With Writing Life, creating an account and converting your file are both free (Kobo uses ePub exclusively). Like KDP, Kobo offers a 70/30 royalty rate, assuming you meet two requirements:

1. Your book is priced between $1.99 and $12.99 (if your book is sold in the United States).

2. The e-book price is at least 20 percent less than the print book, if a print book exists.

Somewhat inconveniently, to access these terms of service you have to either do an Internet search specifically for the Kobo terms of service or begin the registration process—there does not appear to be a link to it on the website—but you are able to cancel the registration if desired. To date, the saturation of Kobo readers in the United States is limited, but worldwide it is the third most popular device and growing. If you have your eye on international sales, working with Kobo is likely in your future.

As you mull over your options for e-book companies, it is best to read all of the fine print (and there is quite a bit) for each company. You need to weigh convenience, ease of use, and the financials before making a decision. Is it better to pay an up-front fee and keep all your profits, or divide your royalties in exchange for free setup? To get the deal that fits you best, you will need to crunch the numbers. It may come down to how many books you believe you can sell, what level of convenience you are looking for, and whether you can make back the cost of an up-front fee.

Troubleshooting Your E-book Experience

Making an e-book is almost too easy, as there are few mechanisms in place to prevent you from publishing before you fully understand what you are doing. For the most part, avoiding the most common mistakes is a matter of taking your time and not rushing the process. Yes, you can upload an unedited, unformatted Word document and get an e-book in return, but would anyone buy it? As has been the message throughout this book, your reputation is on the line; don't mess it up by cutting corners.

So what can you do to make your e-book better than thousands of others out there? Here are some tips:

◆ Have your manuscript professionally edited and designed.

◆ Let your designer know in advance that you plan to publish an e-book.

◆ Read the fine print regarding how you get paid and how your e-book company gets paid. Make sure you understand what you are getting.

◆ If you are formatting your manuscript yourself, take the time to read all of the directives provided by your chosen company. Smashwords and Nook Press provide extensive information to help you avoid setbacks during conversion.

◆ If you're not confident about your ability to format your Word document correctly, hire someone to do it for you. Again, Smashwords has excellent resources to help you find a vendor who will do this for not a lot of money. If you are working with a professional book designer, that person should be able to format the document appropriately.

◆ Make sure that you are able to check the quality of the conversion before the e-book is released.

You must also recognize that the list price for e-books—especially self-published e-books—has been pushed artificially low. This has no doubt contributed to the number of books published without more than a cursory edit. However, if you have read this book this far, you have almost certainly put quality first, and that's great news. For you, the secret to making a profit is selling in volume. And to do that, you need excellent marketing—the subject of the next chapter.

– – – – – –

Choosing a printer, distributor, or e-book company is a major decision that requires a lot of research. Each book project is different, which means you have to customize your decisions to your particular situation. As you work through the selection process, read as much as you can about each vendor until you find the one that's right for you. If you hope to sell your book, you have to focus on making a professional-quality book that stands up to the competition. These vendors are the last link in the chain that will help you achieve that goal.

AVOIDING THE POTHOLE

Understand the Copyright Page

As with printing and binding, the copyright page of a traditionally published book is handled almost entirely by the publishing house. Traditionally published authors don't have much to worry about here. Self-publishers have more at stake. The copyright page functions as a legal document, and authors/publishers need to ensure that their information is inscrutable.

The information contained on a standard copyright page comes from a variety of sources. Besides the copyright notice itself, you may see the Library of Congress Cataloging-in-Publication data, the International Standard Book Number (ISBN), and credits for the people involved in the creation of the book. You may also find acknowledgments for excerpted material or a disclaimer. If you're self-publishing, before you go to print you need to know which of these elements apply to you and how to handle them. This section explains each.

REGISTERING COPYRIGHT

The first element that requires your attention is the copyright notice. While it's true that you hold an inherent copyright to your work just for the fact that you wrote it, should anyone try to infringe on your copyright you will be best served by registering your work with the US Copyright Office (www.copyright.gov). That may sound intimidating, but it is actually a fairly straightforward process. You can register either online or with a paper application, and the applications come with easy-to-understand instructions. The filing fee (as of 2014) is $35 for online registration and $65 for hard copy. In addition to these two requirements, the application and the filing fee, you will be asked to provide a copy of the "deposit"—what the Copyright Office calls the work to be registered. If you file electronically, you can send an electronic file or a hard copy of your manuscript; file a paper application, and you have to send a hard copy. (The Copyright Office prefers online applications, but you are not bound by that.)

It is important to note that when you apply for copyright, you are making a public record. That means anyone can view the information you supply. The Copyright Office website offers some pointed advice on this matter:

> Personally identifying information, such as your address, telephone number, and email address, that is submitted on the registration application becomes part of the public record. Some information will be viewable in the Copyright Office's online databases that are available on the Internet. For this reason, you should provide only the information requested. Please do NOT provide any additional personal information that is not requested, such as your social security number or your driver's license number.

As identity theft is a real problem, heeding this advice only makes sense.

Do You Need to Preregister?

The Copyright Office provides the option of "preregistration" for works that have not yet been completed. (This is separate from registration of unpublished works.) The fee for this service is a whopping $115. I suspect this fee is intended to be a deterrent, as even the Copyright Office notes that preregistration is not helpful for most people. Rather, preregistration is recommended only for those who meet these two criteria: (1) you think it is likely someone will infringe on your copyright before the work is made public, and (2) the work isn't finished. Note also that even if you preregister, you will still need to go through the registration process. Except in extreme circumstances, you will most likely want to *register* your work, rather than preregister it.

You can register your book either before or after publication. Although simple, it can be a lengthy process, and getting the certificate can take nearly three months for electronic applications and nearly six months for paper applications. During particularly busy times, those lags can be even longer. The good news is, unless you have reason to believe that you will *not* be granted copyright, you don't have to wait until you receive your certificate to publish the work. The date of registration is the date the office receives the completed application, not the date you receive your certificate. Still, copyright registration is not something you want to let slip through the cracks. I would recommend beginning earlier rather than later, say, when you have your manuscript back from copyediting. Upon publication, if you have a print book, you will need to send a hard copy to be held in the Library of Congress. For more on that and answers to nearly every other conceivable copyright question, refer to the Copyright Office website.

Formatting Your Copyright Notice

Your copyright notice belongs on the reverse of the title page in your book. You need to include the word "Copyright" or the symbol "©," the year of publication, and your name, in that order. Some publishers choose to use both the word and the symbol for copyright as well as the word "by," but that is not strictly necessary. Examples follow:

© 2014 Katherine Pickett

Copyright © 2014 by Katherine Pickett

LIBRARY OF CONGRESS CATALOGING-IN-PUBLICATION DATA

Most books published by major publishers carry Library of Congress Cataloging-in-Publication data. You will recognize this as

Do Not Fake Your CIP Data!

A surprising number of authors create their own version of a CIP notice and place it on their copyright page, complete with the "Cataloging-in-Publication Data" heading. Presumably they are unaware of the proper procedures for obtaining this information. Do not make this same mistake. Proper CIP data is supplied directly from the Library of Congress and should be formatted exactly as it is supplied to you.

the block of information that begins with the author's name and birth year and includes a list of topics covered in the book. This is for US publishers only and only for books that are likely to be carried by libraries. According to the Library of Congress:

> A Cataloging in Publication record (aka CIP data) is a bibliographic record prepared by the Library of Congress for a book that has not yet been published. When the book is published, the publisher includes the CIP data on the copyright page, thereby facilitating book processing for libraries and book dealers.

Authors publishing as individuals, without setting up a publishing entity, are excluded from the CIP program. If you have set up your own company, however, and expect your books to be carried nationally by libraries, you can begin your quest for CIP data on the Library of Congress website, www.loc.gov. A Library of Congress Control Number (LCCN) may be supplied in lieu of the CIP data for some publishers if their books do not qualify for the CIP.

The Library of Congress is only now beginning to accept e-books for cataloging, with the stipulation that the book be offered in print format as well. Check the website for the latest on these procedures, as they are in flux and most likely will be for some time.

THE ISBN

International Standard Book Numbers (ISBNs) are obtained through R.R. Bowker (www.bowker.com), the official source for ISBNs in the United States. In general, you need a separate ISBN for each edition of your book, including the different formats you choose to create. That means the hardcover, paperback, audio, and e-book versions of your project will each have a different ISBN. You can purchase one ISBN for $125 (as of 2014) or ten for $250. For most people, buying in bulk makes sense, as they may want to publish another book or perhaps separate chapters of the current work as e-books at some point in the future.

You may have seen the notation ISBN-10 and ISBN-13 in certain books. This dual system is the result of a change in the issuance of ISBNs that occurred about ten years ago. For a time, publishers used both formats as a way to bridge the conversion from ten digits to thirteen. As a new publisher, you need only list the thirteen-digit ISBN.

Some authors choose to forgo an ISBN. If you wish to sell your book through a bookstore, however, you will need one, as bookstores use ISBNs to track inventory. You also need an ISBN if you want to be listed in Bowker's Books in Print, which makes your book easier for bookstores to find. Furthermore, having an ISBN demonstrates a professionalism that is helpful when you are trying to persuade readers that your book is of high quality.

CREDITS

You may wish to include a list of credits for the people involved in the creation of your book. This is separate from the acknowledgments and often includes the credits for interior and cover design as well as any photography or drawings. If you aren't sure how to format the credits, ask your vendors how they want their names

and company names to appear. Credits for artwork are usually supplied when permission is granted. It is generally best to follow the format as supplied.

DISCLAIMERS

Various types of books, both fiction and nonfiction, carry disclaimers. While you can have your disclaimer in the front or back matter, often it fits well on the copyright page. Authors of books that offer medical or legal advice generally wish to include a disclaimer to safeguard themselves from any legal action. Fiction writers also may include a disclaimer noting that all people and events in the book are fictional. If you feel you need a disclaimer, speak to a literary attorney to discuss the best wording.

ACKNOWLEDGMENTS FOR USING EXCERPTS

If you do not include them on an acknowledgments page, you may list any acknowledgments for using excerpted material on your copyright page. When you receive permission to use material, most often the grantor of the use also gives some instruction on how to credit the original source (similar to the artwork credits). This usually includes the title of the book, the author, the name of the copyright holder, the copyright year, and specific language for the permission. If you have received such instructions, follow them carefully. If no such instructions were given, choose a standard format. The following example is sufficient:

> The excerpt on page 57 is from *Perfect Bound: How to Navigate the Book Publishing Process Like a Pro* by Katherine Pickett. Copyright © 2014 by Katherine Pickett. Reprinted by permission.

If space on the copyright page is limited, a separate page with the heading "Credits" or "Acknowledgments" may be inserted at

the end of the book. The format for the acknowledgment remains the same.

Having a correctly formatted copyright page is important for two main reasons. One, it carries your copyright notice, which gives you legal protection in the case of someone using your work without permission. And two, it's another way to help make your book look professional. On both counts, your reputation and credibility as an author/publisher are improved when you know how to present your copyright page.

Mapping Out Your Road to Success

Read the fine print when investigating printers, distributors, and e-book companies and don't give in to high-pressure sales tactics.

Crunch the numbers to find the combination of printing, distribution, and/or e-book conversion and distribution that is right for your book.

Register your copyright with the US Copyright Office and gather any other information that will appear on your copyright page.

Have your printer and designer coordinate with one another to ensure your book publishes the way you expect.

8

Getting Used to Self-Promotion
Marketing and Publicity

Although we often think of marketing as what comes after a book has been published, in truth, for the endeavor to be successful, marketing needs to be integrated into the whole process. It is an ongoing effort that grows slowly during the writing and production process, ramps up at publication, and then tapers off to a steady push for the life of the book. Therefore, the launch of your marketing campaign will likely take place somewhere near the end of the production process in anticipation of publication.

Here again you are reminded that it takes more than just strong writing skills to be a successful author. You need a high-quality book and you need to be a savvy promoter as well. The greater your visibility, the better your chances of selling books, and that means capitalizing on traditional forms of media as well as some outlets that are less often considered. The ubiquitous social media sites and other online opportunities are also a must for getting your message—and your book— in front of your readers. Because marketing inherently requires you to make yourself vulnerable, the Pothole for this chapter is about recovering from rejection. Rejection touches

Authors of all stripes have access to a variety of venues for marketing and promoting their books. A broad approach ensures you the greatest visibility.

every writer at some point. The challenge is knowing how to move forward in the face of it.

It is not within the scope of this book to cover all you need to know when you go to market your book. You will find a plethora of books, websites, and online forums dedicated to this topic, and many good ones are listed in the Resources section. I strongly encourage you to review these resources to glean as much information as you can on the art of marketing and promotion. In this chapter I invite you to get your feet wet and start thinking about all that is possible.

TRADITIONAL MARKETING OUTLETS

Over the decades that modern advertisement has been in practice, some reliable forms of marketing have taken root. Print media, television, and radio all offer different benefits for those seeking exposure for their books. Readers of newspapers and magazines may differ from viewers of morning television, and those TV viewers in turn differ from listeners of radio programs. To ensure the greatest exposure possible, make an effort to explore all three of these realms, and take advantage of as many opportunities for media coverage as you can. The more you are seen and the more your name comes up in relation to your field, genre, or book title, the bigger your marketing platform becomes. "Make your goal to become and remain as visible as you can in as many ways as you can," advises author-agent Michael Larsen. "Your sales will reflect your visibility."

Approaching the media can be a little scary if you haven't done it before. To be successful, you need to do three things well: (1) come up with a pitch, (2) contact the right person, and (3) follow up. Self-publishers generally have a more difficult time garnering media attention than do authors with a publishing house behind them, I suspect because the quality of self-published books is so hit or miss. But I'm a firm believer in aiming high, dreaming big, casting a wide net, and all those other sayings that mean the only way to land a really great gig is to make it known that you want the

Defining Marketing, Publicity, and Promotion

The terms *marketing, publicity,* and *promotion* are often used interchangeably. While the three work together, they are not the same. Very briefly:

Marketing is the name for an overarching campaign to get a product in front of consumers.

Publicity refers to a mention in the media.

Promotion is what you do to try to get publicity.

To put the terms in context, your marketing campaign may include a speaking engagement (promotion) for which you receive a write-up in the local paper (publicity). You can control promotion. For the most part, publicity is up to the media.

gig. So research the right person to contact, find out how you can help that person while also getting your book mentioned, and then make the pitch. If you don't hear anything right away, follow up.

Once you have the gig, prepare what you want to say—and don't forget to mention the name of your book! Most of all, do not limit yourself with preconceived notions about who gets media exposure. When it comes to a well-crafted, professional-quality book with a pinpointed audience and marketing hook, even new authors can land a TV interview or a newspaper write-up. Dive in!

Print Media

Newspapers, magazines, and journals. Who reads print anymore? Although the readership is shrinking, with more people choosing the Internet for news and entertainment, print is still a powerful marketing outlet. Particularly if you have a well-defined niche or are writing genre fiction (mystery, romance, or fantasy, for example), these publications may be a solid way to get your book in front of readers. One of the big benefits of print is that it hangs around, gets passed from reader to reader, and can be referred to later. Securing one mention in print can have lasting effects for your visibility. Don't dismiss print as a viable place for publicity.

One lesson with print media is to aim high. You might be tempted to go to a small local newspaper first and then take that mention to the bigger guys to say, "Look at me. I'm newsworthy." I have been told that this is probably the wrong approach. Newspapers and magazines want to break the story. If you feel that you have a chance with the bigger names, start there. If you don't get a bite on that line, move on to the smaller publications. You may have more success with niche publications, but it's not necessary to limit yourself from the start.

To get a favorable response, it is essential that you contact the right person. Research which department is most appropriate for your book topic and try to get the name of the person you want to reach. You might first look to the book reviewer, but don't stop there. Newspapers and magazines have special sections for a variety of events and topics. If you can sell your book as pertaining to one of these topics—for example, sports, weddings, society, or local celebrity—then approach that editor. Tell him or her what you think is newsworthy about your project and how it can help the publication. Don't be afraid of spin.

Whichever newspaper, magazine, or journal you reach out to, you have to be prepared with a hook. This is not always the hook of your book but rather the hook for the story that you want the publication to run. The possibilities are far-reaching, but consider that you may want to *make news* rather than try to sell yourself *as the news*. An example of making news might be interviewing someone well known in the field or offering solutions to a common problem the publication's readers may face. This is opposed to simply saying you wrote a book, which would be selling yourself. When you make your pitch, focus on the benefits for the editor and the publication. Author Bob Baker addresses this issue in his highly readable e-book *Mega Book Publicity: 5 Steps to Getting Free Media Exposure for Your Books*. "Whenever you communicate with someone—whether on the Internet, in person, on the phone, or in writing—he or she is either consciously or unconsciously asking, 'So what's in this for me, bub?' Your job is to answer that unspoken question and deliver something of value." Once you make your pitch, be sure to follow up. That final step can be the difference between getting the media op and missing it.

Television

The medium of television can be intimidating for authors who are used to sitting at a computer for long hours by themselves. Yet it is a great way to get exposure for your book. Just having the cover of your book shown on the screen for a few seconds can improve sales. Suddenly, viewer-readers know not only your face, name, and personality but also what the cover of your book looks like, so they will know it when they see it online or at the bookstore.

Obviously, the bigger the station or show you can land a spot on, the greater the impact on sales, but local television can be powerful, too, especially for new authors. Nearly every city has an around-the-town segment during one of its daily news broadcasts; some have whole shows dedicated to city-specific events. Look for some timely event that relates to your book and contact the station to see if you can get on its show. A book such as *Derek Jeter: The Quiet Leader* may be pitched in time for the opening of spring training or in relation to World Leadership Day. A novel set in World War II may be profiled on D-Day, VE Day, or another anniversary related to the war. Don't know what designation might fit your book? You're in luck. Entire books and websites are available that describe special designations for every day of the year. *Chase's Calendar of Events* from McGraw-Hill, for example, offers an exhaustive list of famous birthdays, death anniversaries, historical events, and every kind of "day" you can think of—from Groundhog Day to Flag Day to World Day of Bullying Prevention. May, it turns out, is Gifts from the Garden Month, perfect for selling *Growing and Cooking with Flax*. That may seem obscure, but it gives you an in, a hook, and that's all you need to make your story relevant and newsworthy for small-market television. This practice works for all forms of media, but local television seems to be the most open to this sort of marketing/entertainment.

Perhaps the thought of being seen by all of your friends and family, not to mention the rest of the city or region, frightens you. The best cure I know for this is preparation. Practice in the shower. Practice in front of the mirror. Practice in front of friends and family. Get so that you can speak succinctly about your book and sound relaxed while doing it. I recall being so nervous about giving a talk in front of my high school class that I didn't even begin to prepare. The whole concept was just too frightening. As expected, my presentation was terrible. Many years later, when I was scheduled to give a talk to a writing group, I was lucky enough to have a husband with great speaking skills who encouraged me—forced me—to practice. And what a difference that made. Now I am able to give talks in front of large audiences and small, and I get compliments on my presentation abilities. The reason is that I got over my fear just enough to be able to prepare and slowly build up my comfort level. If you really feel that you are lacking in this area, consider hiring a coach or joining an organization like Toastmasters. Especially for those authors who hope to add speaking tours to their repertoire as experts in their field, professional advice may be worth the expense.

ROADSIDE ASSISTANT

Emily Ayala
Author

Emily Ayala is the coauthor of *The St. Louis Wedding Book: Two Sisters' Guide to Your Ultimate Wedding*, written with her sister Allison Hockett. Together the self-publishing sisters appeared on two television news shows and had a full-page write-up of their book in the *St. Louis Post-Dispatch*.

How did you come up with the marketing hook of a St. Louis wedding guide?
Allison once heard the three ladies who wrote *Girlfriends on the Go* speak about their book, which was a local guide to finding places to go with friends around St. Louis. They had much success, so we thought it would be a great business plan to write another

local book. Since we both planned weddings here in St. Louis, we thought this city needed something of this sort.

Our marketing ideas were clearer because our niche was so small, being a local guide and only targeting people who are getting married. Because we featured local businesses, we thought our first plan of action was to have our vendors sell our book. We also contacted all the bridal shows around town to see if we could have a booth to sell our books (which didn't work as well as we thought it would). The media enjoyed our story, since we are two local sisters who grew up in St. Louis.

When it came time to market your book, what was the most difficult part about approaching the media?
Probably the most difficult part about contacting the media is the fear of rejection. We decided to take the easy approach and send press releases via e-mail first before contacting them by phone. We thought, this way we aren't putting them on the spot. Actually, it worked great. We got a huge response—partly because our book is local. My biggest advice is to find the specific person that handles your type of stories. Example: Contact the producer and not the news anchor.

Do you have any advice for new authors regarding marketing?

◆ Be thinking of marketing well before writing your book. Marketing is probably the hardest part.

◆ Don't be afraid to try everything!

◆ Be specific on who you contact. Don't send out blanket press releases to everyone. Personalize each one depending on whom you are contacting.

◆ Spend little to no money at first.

What was the most rewarding part about writing a book?
Probably the obvious—to hold it in your hands and to say to yourself and everyone that you finished a book. It took us years of on and off work, so to finally see the finished project was magic. Not many people can say that they wrote a book.

Radio

Approaching radio stations is much like approaching print publications and television: make sure that you are contacting the right person, go in with an angle, and then follow up. Again, local programs will be easier to get on, but if you have a book with national appeal, you might give it a go with the bigger names.

Radio does present some drawbacks compared to other media. For example, no one gets to see your book cover. You may also have to do more preparation regarding what you are going to say, taking care to avoid the language crutches that may go unnoticed in television. Keep the "ums," "likes," and "you knows" to a minimum. But there are many benefits to radio, too. You don't have to worry about your appearance, for starters. The radio show is also likely to say your name multiple times leading up to the interview. Finally, you are able to connect with people who don't read print or watch television, and those who do catch you in multiple formats are more likely to remember you and your book.

For all forms of media, timing is everything. Become familiar with the calendars for the various outlets you want to reach. Some television programs set their calendars a month in advance; some print publications set their calendars four to six months in advance. Self-publishers may wish to keep that in mind when planning their release date. That said, it can pay off to approach a media editor just before a deadline. Print publications may find themselves with a hole to fill and will jump on your proposed article. Television shows, too, may have airtime they need to fill quickly. Although it is rare for a major or national show to have last-minute openings, producers of the midmorning program on your local television station may decide that you are just what they need for the next broadcast.

IN-PERSON MARKETING

In-person events offer you a way to connect with potential readers that traditional media appearances don't. The time that you put into locating and defining your audience will pay dividends now, as you will know where to find appropriate events when you are ready for them. A strong marketing hook will add to your appeal as an invited speaker. Opportunities for in-person marketing include giving a book talk to relevant groups; attending and participating in conferences, conventions, and workshops; and discussing your book with readers in a book club setting. If you become a polished speaker, personal appearances may develop into another revenue stream for you.

Speaking Engagements

Although book signings, especially for traditional publishers, have lost their luster—the return on investment just isn't there—speaking engagements are still an important venue for selling yourself and your book. For nonfiction writers, the really good thing about these events is that you can show off what an expert you are in your field. Simply having your name on a book helps you to be perceived as an expert. When you then give a polished talk on the subject, not to mention show off how incredibly personable and knowledgeable you are, you will be set up to sell the most books.

Fiction authors may wonder how they can take advantage of this format. Besides the general fans of your work, you may be surprised by how many people want to hear what you did to get published. Others want to get to know your personality. They want to know what inspired you to write the story that captured their attention. Authors who write for a cause are prized at the organizations surrounding the cause. Children's fiction authors Tim Hill and Angela Ruzicka, for example, speak to grade schools and advocacy groups. Barbara Davis, the author of *Darkside of Debonair*, a romance/adventure novel, has presented to groups to raise awareness about the bushmeat trade in Africa, a central focus of her novel. The trick is to find the people most interested in your topic, locate the person in charge of special events, and offer to speak to their organization. Then follow up to secure the engagement.

Unlike television or radio, where your audience may or may not be receptive to your message, with speaking engagements you can bet that most of the audience is rooting for you. They want a great presentation; they want to learn about you and hear what you have to say. If you can relax a little, you will be able to make a personal connection with the audience and everyone will have a good time—including you!

One question that often comes up with this sort of event is whether you should remind the audience that your book is for sale at the back of the room. Different people have different styles. If you can get the emcee for the event to make that announcement, that is the best position to be in. If not, go ahead and mention the books. That's why you're there. Just keep it brief: "Thank you for having me tonight. If you're interested in purchasing a copy of *Derek Jeter: The Quiet Leader*, copies are available on the back table. Good night!" I recommend not including the price in your announcement. It reminds listeners that you're making a sales pitch, not just being helpful.

Conferences and Workshops

Marketing at conferences and workshops is different from marketing at other venues. You may have more time to make your pitch to the other attendees, and the soft sell tends to work better than the hard sell. As with most speaking engagements, the conferences and workshops that you will be attending will be based in your area of interest. That means you already have something in common with your prospective buyers. Whether you opt to have a booth or simply attend, however, there are some fairly simple guidelines for making the most out of these opportunities.

First, bring business cards, bookmarks, or other small handouts to exchange. You can't always tell from a conference website if there will be networking time, but for the most part you can assume there will be. Even if there isn't a designated networking segment, any conversation you have may result in your companion becoming an interested reader.

Second, wear a name tag. Be sure to add "author" after your name, or be even more bold and wear a tag that says "Ask me about my book." This can be an easy conversation starter, welcome at nearly any conference or workshop you may attend. After all, who isn't trying to dream up a topic of conversation when standing around in a room full of strangers?

On Book Signings

Arranging a book signing can take a lot of time and effort, and you aren't likely to sell more than a few books. That is why traditional publishers have lost interest. Self-publishers, however, still like to work this angle. Whether these authors receive adequate return on investment is up for debate, but with the right book in the right location, it might be. If nothing else, the event gets your name out there and keeps you engaged with marketing. Some independent bookstores and cafés like to host these events for local authors, whether they are independently or traditionally published. It gives the venue an air of intellectuality, and it gets people into the store. Of course, these people won't all be book buyers. Many will be your friends and family stopping by to show their support. Still, if you have always wanted to do a book signing, try it out. Just know that you may spend more time thanking people you know for showing up than you will signing books for your adoring fans.

And third, as is true whenever you are networking, you must be sincere in your conversations with fellow attendees. They did not come to this event to be sold something. If you get the feeling that you can sell your book right there, do it; but you may find greater success in having the person contact you outside of the conference. Arrange a phone call or direct him or her to your website. Generally speaking, you are trying to get leads and exposure, not actual sales, when you are at a conference.

Book Clubs

The book club has become a popular if nontraditional venue for promotion. How do you capitalize on it? Give contact information at the back of your book, on social media, and on your website, and invite readers to contact you regarding speaking to their group. Ideally everyone in the group will read—and buy—your book. Then you meet the group on discussion day, either in person or by phone or video. That small group of people will have already purchased your book, so you won't be selling anything to them unless you have another book in the series. By being friendly and accessible, however, you will build your name recognition and reputation. Further, the book club members will tell their friends about you and the book, and that's valuable. Word of mouth continues to be one of the most reliable forms of marketing.

BUILDING AN ONLINE PRESENCE

By now you've probably heard it a hundred times: you need to leverage the Internet and social media if you want to build your author platform and sell your books. Indeed, skipping the Internet is a mistake. I firmly believe that without an online presence, you might as well not exist for your readers. What does it mean to have an online presence? In his e-book *Mega Book Publicity*, Bob Baker writes, "You have a strong presence online when a growing number of people who have an interest in your topic or genre keep finding you in the places where they spend time online." That means providing solid content and disseminating it to the sites that appeal to your target market. But with so many sites available to you, how do you know which ones to choose? More important, how do you make them work for you? In this section we'll cover the most important actions for you to take to increase your visibility online and make sure your readers can find you and your book.

Author Websites

Both traditionally published and self-published authors benefit from author websites. If you're a really big name, your publisher will supply this site for you. For the other 99 percent, this is the author's responsibility. And although you can build your website yourself for not a lot of money, it can be tricky and extremely time-consuming. If you aren't tech savvy, have limited time, or don't have an eye for design, you are probably better off hiring a web designer.

But is having an author website really worth paying someone to design and host it? The answer is yes. A site dedicated to you and your books can act as the foundation of your Internet presence. To use another metaphor, think of it as the hub of the wheel you are creating, so that all the followers and friends and fans you gather at other sites across the Internet, along with those you meet through your in-person events, have a central place to go to learn more about you and how to buy your book. To have effective online marketing, you need that central location—that hub—where your readers can find you.

Use your author site to tell readers about yourself, describe your books, tout positive reviews, sell your books or link to a site that does sell your books, and advertise any upcoming events you'll be attending or hosting. Be sure to include an image of the cover of your book and provide links to every other website where you can be found online, such as your blog, Twitter, Facebook, LinkedIn, or Goodreads. You can also link to the blogs and websites of other respected people in your field, relevant articles, and helpful tips—any content that you think your readers will benefit from and enjoy. If you have an e-mail newsletter, use your website to capture e-mail addresses. Being able to contact your readers directly via a newsletter—and more important, a newsletter that they have signed up for—can be a powerful marketing tool. Take a peek at other author sites for more ideas. If your site is done right, it will convey the tone of your genre and book while giving you an immediate air of professionalism.

Author Blogs

Although they aren't a surefire connection to purchasers, blogs have proven very effective for many authors, both of fiction and of nonfiction. In fact, a number of blog writers have turned their blogs into books or, as was the case for the blog *Julie and Julia*, into movies. When blogs do work, it is usually because the blogger offers *consistent* and *consistently good* content. That means writing more than just once every month or two; blogging weekly or even daily is ideal. When you provide engaging stories and consistently high quality information, blog followers begin to turn to you for their news and entertainment. In this way, a blog can be an effective means to bring readers to your marketing hub.

Right now you may be thinking that there is no way you can keep up with a daily or weekly blog. Three factors can make the challenge less daunting. One, effective blog posts tend to be short, somewhere between 350 and 1,000 words. Two, if you keep to a schedule, blog writing becomes routine rather than a new adventure each time you begin a post. And three, you can write several blog posts all at once—say, on Monday you write three short posts and one long post—and then schedule them to be published throughout the week or month. This feature offers you much more flexibility in how and when you write.

One very attractive aspect to keeping a blog is that there isn't a monetary commitment. Two of the largest and most popular blog hosts, WordPress.com and Blogger, allow you to create your account and run your blog at no cost. They are also fairly easy to navigate, as far as getting your blog up and running, with plenty of information on the Help pages if you get stuck. You just fill out some profile information, choose the name for your blog, select a design template (which you can change at any time), and begin typing. As for content, you have to be creative. Take your prompts from a variety of sources related to your field, and then express an opinion. You can also write about your writing process or events that you have attended. Include photos, videos, links, and lists to keep your readers interested. Also consider arranging guest posts, to put your readers in touch with other professionals and personalities in your field.

Keeping a blog takes time, but this is definitely one medium where, if you're going to do it, you had better do it right or you

How Easy Is WordPress.com?

Not sure whether you'd be able to figure out how to run a blog even if you wanted to? Here's how easy it is: One day I received a phone call from a blogger who needed someone to edit her blog posts. Although I had never edited a blog before, after we discussed what she needed, I agreed to give it a try. That night I went to WordPress.com to teach myself as much as I could about how to run a blog. That was the advent of *The POP Newsletter*. I had a post up that night. The next day I was prepared for the first assignment from the new client, and I had learned how to set up, post to, and edit a blog in less than twenty-four hours.

are wasting your efforts. Put in the time to be a good and reliable blogger and you will reap the rewards.

Amazon Book Profiles

If you're being published by someone else, the book profiles on Amazon will be filled out for you. Amazon imports the data from various sources, and traditional publishers take care to ensure that all of the requested information is complete and accurate. Self-publishers must do this task themselves. Although it might seem like busywork to verify, fill out, and correct the numerous fields, it's important to have a complete and accurate profile for your book.

While these pages are crucial for getting your book found in an Internet search, there are other, possibly more important benefits as well. When readers locate a book only to find an incomplete profile, they ask themselves why. The first possibility is that the book is no longer available. The second is that this book was self-published—and by an amateur. Neither of these impressions helps you sell books. That means that while potential buyers looked for and found your book—a self-publisher's hurdle in itself—you did not capitalize on having caught their attention, and your marketing efforts were for naught.

The most essential fields for you to complete are the book title and author, the book cover, the price and formatting information, and the book description. You should also be sure to select the "Search Inside" feature; this is not an automatic setting. Providing information about yourself is encouraged, as is listing any endorsements or professional reviews you were able to obtain. More than likely you already know that you need reader reviews as well. Don't be afraid to ask around for these. They are an important cog in the machine that helps you climb the ranks on Amazon. It's not entirely clear how—Amazon won't tell—but the number of good reviews you receive seems to be incorporated into the site's algorithm for ranking books. The better the rank, the higher your book is listed on the search page and, hopefully, the more books you sell.

Amazon also allows authors to inform readers about themselves and their books through Amazon Author Pages. This is different from the book profile and is something a publishing house

Asking for Reviews

To get reviews and endorsements for your book, you may have to ask outright. Whom do you ask? Start with colleagues and acquaintances who have read the book. Send copies to influential people in your field or genre and ask them to review it. Also invite your fans and followers on social media sites. Then contact bloggers who write on your topic or in your subgenre. The Amazon Top Reviewers, people who have reviewed hundreds if not thousands of books and had their reviews marked "helpful," may also agree to review your book. Other sources include *Self-Publishing Review*, *Midwest Book Review*, and *Kirkus Reviews*. Some places, like *Kirkus*, charge a fee; others are free. (You can find contact information for these sites in the Resources.) Of course, there is a caveat: Just because someone agrees to review your book does not mean that you will receive a positive review. Your best bet for heading off a negative review? Publish a great book.

likely will not complete for you, yet you should take advantage of this opportunity. Improve your online visibility by including your photo, a biography, and a list of your books. You can also import your blog and list upcoming events. Find more information via Author Central (https://authorcentral.amazon.com).

SELECTING THE SOCIAL MEDIA SITES THAT ARE RIGHT FOR YOU

Throughout the previous section we talked about building a foundation for your online persona. Now it is time to interact with your audience, and social media is a great way to do that. The goal with social media is to be found in the places that your readers visit. This requires knowing who your target market is and where these people spend their time online. The research you did into your target audience early on will be of great help now.

Some key guidelines apply to all forms of social media. First, no matter what your privacy settings may be, it's best to assume that anything you post online is public. Second, except in certain places that encourage it, you must not engage in the hard sell. People are turned off by this and will unfriend you, unfollow you, or otherwise tune you out because of it. You must first become a participant. Then you can begin the self-promotion. This is one reason why having an author website is helpful: you don't need to sell your book outright on social media; you need only to entice people to your site, where you can make your pitch and they can buy your book.

So how do you choose the sites to join? It helps to know the culture and mode of interaction that are attendant with the various sites. Each one offers something slightly different, and you will find that some make sense to you right away while others remain a mystery. Participating in the sites that you understand will be more enjoyable and therefore more likely to produce results for you. Why? Because you won't mind putting in a little time to become part of the community. That is crucial to your success.

Now let's discuss some of the most popular sites, how they differ, and how you as an author can use them to the greatest effect.

Facebook

For a number of years now, Facebook has been the be-all and end-all of social media. Indeed, in 2013 the site topped *1.5 billion* users worldwide. As an author it's hard to ignore its potential for reaching readers. Once you join, you have two choices: use your personal page for your author persona or create an author/book page. Many authors use both, with the plan of keeping their personal page personal and their author/book page public. This doesn't seem to work as well as one would hope, however, and many of the authors I know have ended up choosing one and sticking to it. You may wish to do the same. Given recent changes that restrict how many people see posts to business pages, even for those who have "liked" it (some experts estimate only 10 percent of people who liked your page will actually see your posts in their newsfeed), it may make more sense to use your personal page to reach the most readers.

Facebook can be a great way to promote upcoming events or show off successes you have achieved. You can also use Facebook to give away books and interact with your fans. Through its group pages, Facebook offers a way to engage with your target market and become active in the community. Find groups by typing your area of interest plus "group" in the search field and investigating what comes up. Facebook will also suggest groups you may like to join based on those you already belong to. Most participants are not looking for someone to come in and start selling them something, however. In fact, some groups will ban you as a spammer if you try this. As is often the case, you must build a rapport before you can market your wares with credibility.

Many self-publishers have asked about buying an advertisement through Facebook. The return on investment with these ads is unclear. You can get one for just a few dollars a day, but most people tend not to click on them. The ads do allow you to display the cover of your book, however, so that when readers see it again elsewhere, they will (hopefully) remember it.

Facebook is an important site to engage in, in part because your readers will expect you to have a presence there. Yet, it can be a struggle to be heard, and Facebook has made it more difficult, rather than less, for authors and others to get noticed. Participating in relevant groups and joining the community to connect with your readers will be more effective than waiting for them to find you.

ROADSIDE ASSISTANT

Mich Hancock
Social media expert

Mich Hancock is the owner of 100th Monkey Media, a social media company that specializes in developing, creating, and managing a social media presence for local and nationwide businesses. She shares some of her insights on using social media to sell books.

What are some common mistakes you have seen from authors using social media?
Social media has become the way we market. Your compelling message can reach more people in a quicker manner than ever before. That said, it does not happen overnight, and it definitely takes time and commitment. The main point to keep in mind

is that social media is a conversation. It is not *me yapping at you about my awesome book*. It is me listening, collaborating, building a relationship, and sharing with you.

Ideally, you will begin to build your social media platform sooner rather than later; start while you are writing your book, not after the book is published and ready for purchase. Be willing to take the audience on the journey with you and make them a part of the process. Also, be willing to give away a chapter, a top ten list, a template, and so forth. The old model was to create, market, and sell. Social media is not as linear. Nowadays, audiences need to feel connected to you in a more real way; they must trust you before buying anything from you. They need to pay attention before they'll pay money.

What advice do you have for new authors as far as how to get the most out of social media?

Start with a few platforms and then work your way into others. For example, create a Facebook fan page and Twitter account. Use HootSuite for scheduling posts. Think about the elements you can utilize on each platform and use them! On Facebook, you can use words that call for engagement (answer a question, fill in the blank, and so on), link to online information, and also post an image. You have three elements available; use them to convey a message or stir an emotion. On Twitter, you can use words and links and also a short video via the Vine app.

Other platforms to consider are Pinterest, an online digital pin board for visually sharing, say, your motivating thoughts or perhaps a board inspired by one of your book's characters. Instagram is perfect for sharing pictures and allowing your audience a peek into your world. YouTube allows you to upload quick messages and updates with your audience; share with them what compelled you to write a certain passage, ask for their help when you are experiencing a block, or let them get to know you in a more real way. If your book is for the businessperson, you will definitely want to create a LinkedIn presence. Also consider Google+; it will help you be found! Google+ is the social aspect that connects with all the other Google goodies.

Finally, make sure that all your social media "holds hands." Your web page and e-mail newsletters should include links to all your social media. Where possible, include links on each social media page for other pages. Use hashtags to allow your audience to follow subjects on Twitter, Instagram, and more. Invite people into your world and give them a reason to become a part of all your social media sites.

Twitter

The rules for Twitter are much different from those for Facebook. Most important, you have only 140 characters to express your ideas. To match these shortened messages, postings happen much more rapidly. Whereas on Facebook you may post three to five times a week, some people tweet three to five times a day if not an hour. Tweeting at least a few times throughout the day will help you reach the most people, although it has been shown that consistency and quality of your tweets is more important than quantity.

Because the traffic is so heavy on Twitter, it can be difficult to get noticed, but there are solid ways to gain a following. First, you have to participate. Find the influential people and organizations in your field or genre and follow them. Then, retweet or reply to those posts that you find valuable. Also tweet your own updates at various times throughout the day. As with blogs, providing quality information or entertainment is what will get you noticed. Send out links to your blog posts, other people's blogs and articles, and photos, and keep it relevant to your genre or field. Soon enough you will have a small gathering of people to follow, and some of those people will follow you back. You can lose followers surprisingly quickly, too, so keep up a regular presence to maintain and grow your community.

Because the information is constantly changing, Twitter can be a real time sink. Luckily, several sites have arisen that allow you to schedule your tweets. Writing and scheduling tweets daily will ensure that your material is fresh. Some popular sites that offer this service include Tweetdeck, Gremln (note there is no *i*), and HootSuite.

It's easy to get overwhelmed on Twitter, so you need to stay organized and focused. Remember, you are looking to build rapport with your target audience. You are encouraged to advertise special events, price reductions, positive reviews, blog posts, and the like. Just don't make self-promotion your first or only tweets.

YouTube

What's the most searched website after Google and Yahoo? That's right: YouTube. For authors, YouTube offers an opportunity to be creative in a different medium. How can you use videos to sell books? Some options include creating a book trailer; videotaping yourself speaking to your audience; recording an interview, either of you or by you, on a topic related to your book; or doing a reading from your work. You may also wish to treat it as a video blog, or vlog, where you make several short videos containing updates, news, funny stories, or any other information you want to share with your readers. (Humor, of course, is subjective; unless you are a natural comedian, tread lightly.) With YouTube, as with many other social media sites, you are tapping into the content marketing movement. You are reaching out to your audience not just to sell books but to connect with readers in a meaningful way. By being visible in yet another location, you are improving your name recognition and gaining exposure for your book.

The most successful YouTube videos tend to be short, say two minutes or less. If you have a topic that might run longer than three or four minutes, consider breaking up the information into multiple videos. To promote these videos, post them to any other social media site you belong to; mention them (and include a link) in a blog post; and e-mail the link with your e-newsletter if you have one. Publishing a series of videos can be powerful in making a name for yourself as an expert and influential figure with your audience.

Not all of your videos need to be directly related to your book. For those that are, take the opportunity to show the cover of your book. In all cases, make it easy for your viewers to find their way to your author website. Subtlety will be appreciated. Provide your web address, with the focus on being helpful rather than promotional.

Goodreads

Although Goodreads was launched less than a decade ago, by 2013 it boasted more than twenty million users and has become a reliable place for authors to get in touch with their readers. Given the focus on books, the benefits to authors may seem obvious, but Goodreads does take some exploring. As always, get involved with the community before trying to sell books. You can find relevant groups by searching for them in the search field; then add to the discussion. These groups not only put you in touch with your target audience but also with your competition. You can find and analyze competing titles and then read the reviews to see how you can improve your own book.

You also have the opportunity to request reviews and offer giveaways in specific sections of the site. Giveaways are a good method for generating reviews, but you can't be certain that the review will be favorable. Goodreads reviewers have a reputation for being harsher than other reviewers, meaning four stars out of five on Goodreads may be equivalent to five stars on Amazon.

Another feature of this site is the Goodreads Author Program, which allows you to create an author profile and share personal data, your web address, a bio, details on upcoming events, and other tidbits your readers may want to know. To join the Author Program, your book has to be published or in the process of being published.

It is essential for authors to be in touch with their audience as well as their competition. Goodreads offers authors a way to do both.

Pinterest

Pinterest is another popular site where you can learn about your readers while also letting them know about you and your book. In the last quarter of 2013, Pinterest was second only to Facebook in referring traffic to other sites. This is valuable when you are trying to attract readers to your online marketing hub.

To engage on this site, create virtual pin boards that relate to your interests, the interests of your characters, or the interests of

Internet Marketing in Action

In researching this book, I asked aspiring author Tyler Johnson for his views on using social media to sell books. He offered a case study of how online marketing and promotion can change people's behavior, using himself as the subject.

> I am currently (kinda) watching WWE [wrestling]. I had long lost interest in it, but I discovered via a running online article that a few of the performers there were totally different on Twitter than they were portrayed on TV. I checked it out and was amazed. These people who came off as stoic, unfriendly, and downright unlikeable had sparkling personalities and razor-sharp wit. I now watch these programs *just* so I have context for their inevitable tweets.
>
> The online article is written by Matt Fowler, an editor on the gaming site IGN.com. This article is basically a weekly blog, called *The Wrestling Wrap-Up*, where the author humorously recaps what has happened in the WWE universe the past week. At the end of each *Wrap-Up*, Fowler has links to his Twitter, Facebook, Tout, and Tumblr accounts. I use this as an example because this weekly article got me to change my behavior in three ways: (1) I now have a Twitter account, (2) I now have a Tumblr account, and (3) I once again watch wrestling.

When you engage your target audience, you build a relationship with them, and that, as Tyler indicated, motivates them to buy whatever it is you're selling.

your readers. Then "pin" the items you find worthwhile to one of your boards and leave a comment. If you are writing fiction, you may choose to use the setting or characters from your book as the focus of what you pin. Nonfiction writers can focus on the topic of their book but may also want to discover the other interests of their readers by following their boards. For a book like *Derek Jeter: The Quiet Leader*, pins of note might be photos with quotes by or about Jeter or a relevant article from his Turn 2 Foundation website.

You will also want to create pins of your own. The pins you create can be a wide range of things—from your own blog posts, craft ideas, and favorite books to new or relevant articles, photos, and products found elsewhere on the Internet. If you include your web address with your pin, Pinterest users will track back to your site to find out more about you and the item you have pinned. When others like your pin, they will pin it themselves and increase your visibility across Pinterest. The more you participate, the more likely you are to be found. If you keep interesting pin boards, you can become a resource for other users for new and novel ideas, books, or products.

There are dozens of other sites for you to explore, and you will find the links and short descriptions of many of them in the Resources. Perhaps most conspicuous by their absence from this list, however, are LinkedIn and Google+. These sites offer even more ways to reach people, and they have slightly different cultures from the other sites listed. LinkedIn is business-oriented, while Google+ emphasizes sharing via circles of friends and colleagues. They aren't so different, however, from Facebook, in that you will get the most out of them by being involved on a regular basis, joining the various groups they offer, and making an effort to get to know the culture of the site before trying to sell anyone your book. Both offer outlets to promote your blogs and videos and provide another way to get in touch with your audience and direct them back to the hub of your network—your author website.

Making the Most of Your Time Online

You now have the highlights of what's available to you for building your online presence and staying visible, and even more information is provided in the Resources. Still, you have to decide how much you want to do. It's a great big Internet out there, and this chapter merely scratches the surface of all the possibilities. So what's the trick? How do you make the most of your time online?

The best advice I received about how to approach social media was this: Pick three things that you can do well and do those. It is difficult to stay involved in more than three of these sites; there is only so much time in the day, and if you aren't able to stay connected, you are wasting the small amount of time that you are dedicating to each site. If you can find the three sites you enjoy and that make sense to you, staying active won't be such a chore and your natural winning personality will shine through.

In choosing your three sites, think also about the demographics of your audience and compare that with who visits the various platforms. YouTube, Instagram, and Reddit tend to be more popular with college-age people and older. Wattpad users have historically been teens and twentysomethings, but the site is gaining ground with people over twenty-five. According to a 2013 Pew Research Center study, "Twitter and Instagram have particular appeal to younger adults, urban dwellers, and non-whites." The same study found that women are four times more likely to be on Pinterest than men, and 23 percent of Internet users over age fifty are on Pinterest. Meanwhile, more than 80 percent of people on social media of any kind are also on Facebook. With more than 1.5 billion people on Facebook, that last statistic isn't so surprising.

Visibility is key to selling your book. Improving your visibility requires a combination of self-driven promotion and media exposure. It is impossible to take advantage of every single opportunity out there, but a broad approach that includes at least some of the traditional marketing venues, in-person events, and a presence online will greatly increase your chances to sell your book. You have spent a significant amount of time, money, and effort creating the best book you can. If you want people to read it, you have to let them know it is available. Whenever you put something out into the world—yourself or your book—you risk rejection, and that can make your promotion efforts intimidating. But when it comes to gaining readership, you will have much more success if you go to your readers instead of waiting for them to find you.

AVOIDING THE POTHOLE
Move Forward After Rejection

Rejection in the publishing industry comes in many forms and can be felt at nearly any stage. Perhaps you never got noticed by an agent. Or your agent was unsuccessful in finding a publisher for your book. Perhaps you experienced the sting of developmental editing as a form of rejection of the concept and ideas you felt so strongly about. Later you may experience the rejection that can come just before and after the book has launched: you receive bad reviews, no one buys the book, and you can't seem to get any traction in your marketing. Most authors go through at least some of these forms of rejection at one time or another. But there are sound ways to deal with them. Most important, you can't wallow. You must recover and push on. Here I offer some steps you can take to stay positive and keep moving forward.

WHEN AGENTS DON'T RESPOND

These days rejection from agents generally comes in the form of silence. A common directive in the submission guidelines for agents reads, "If you haven't heard from us in two to four weeks, you can assume we have decided to pass on your project." Although it is frustrating not to hear back from someone, and although we would all like to find out *why* we were rejected, this method of rejection can be easier to take. You are now free to focus on the next step.

To keep your spirits up during the trying period of looking for an agent, avoid contacting just one or two dream agents at a time and then waiting for a response from each before approaching anyone else. Instead, send out as many targeted queries as you can

(emphasis on *targeted*), make a spreadsheet of contact information and when you should be hearing back from each, and then forget about them. Research new agents, begin writing or revising your manuscript, revamp your query letters and proposals, or take steps toward building your marketing platform. Check your spreadsheet on a set schedule and note who has "decided to pass" on your project. Then send out a new round of queries and begin the process again. If you get any positive responses, print them out and paste them to your wall to help you through the negative ones. Review the positive comments as often as needed.

If after a valiant effort you're ready to give up on agents, remember that there are other avenues open to you. You can approach publishing houses yourself, form a collaboration with a business or nonprofit, or self-publish. You may also consider taking on a coauthor whose strengths complement your weaknesses to make your book a more appealing acquisition, and then approach a new set of agents. Whatever you decide, rejection by an agent is not the end of the publishing road. If you are committed to your project, you can find the right path to publication.

WHEN PUBLISHERS DON'T WANT YOU

If you skipped the agent and decided to contact publishers directly, see the recommendations in the previous section. Your time will be spent much the same way as those authors who are querying agents.

Now, even if you have an agent, it may be a while before you hear anything from publishers. On the occasions when you do get interest, celebrate, tape that letter to your wall—and then come back to reality. "Interest" is not the same as a signed contract, and the publisher or you may still back out. Be prepared for some negotiating and compromising. Either one of you may decide that this is not the best fit, and you will be back to the drawing board. But again, you have plenty of other work to do while you wait.

Many fiction writers report having polished one or two sample chapters for submission but then not having the rest of the manuscript ready to go when someone finally asks to see the whole thing. They find themselves in a scramble. Avoid this by working on revisions while you are querying publishers.

Nonfiction writers may be in a different boat, as they may be waiting for that contract before beginning their manuscripts. But as I have noted throughout this book, writing is only one part of being a successful author. Use this time for networking with appropriate associations and groups, building a following on the Internet, writing articles for trade journals or other appropriate publications, and polishing your proposal in case this contract falls through.

If you find that you are getting a lot of rejections, it may be time to review the proposal or manuscript again and figure out what is not selling it. Have you not presented the hook in the best way? Does the manuscript need revisions that a developmental editor could help you with? Is your market too small for a traditional publisher to be interested? The information on publishing routes presented in Chapter 1 will help you determine if it is time to move on—whether that's to a different publisher, a different route to publication, or a different book idea.

WHEN REVIEWERS WON'T ENDORSE YOU

This type of rejection, in which you get negative comments from reviewers before the book is released to the public at large, can come through two different means. One, you or your publisher may send out page proofs (sent prior to publication, these are often called either bound galleys or uncorrected page proofs) to be reviewed by influential people in your field. Alternatively, finished books, called ARCs (advance reader copies), may be reviewed by periodicals, blogs, or readers through a website such as Goodreads before the book is officially released. These reviewers may be professionals whom you've asked specifically for a

review or average Joes who picked up your book and decided to write about it. Your goal in this process is to get an endorsement or possibly a write-up, depending on who is conducting the review. Whenever someone reviews your book, however, you have to be prepared for bad news.

So, what do you do if you get a bad review during the page proof stage? If you're with a traditional publisher, you might not have a lot of options. The house won't want to pay for major rewrites at this point. If the reviews are scathing, you may be able to finagle some rewriting, or you may have to wait until the book comes out and attempt to have changes made at reprint. If this is you, skip to the next section, "When Readers Won't Buy It." If you are self-publishing and have sent out page proofs for reviews, you will have to decide what approach to take. Are you going to stick by your work, or do you agree with the reviewers and want to make revisions? It's a difficult decision and depends largely on who is reviewing the book, what your own vision for the book is, and what kind of budget and publication schedule you have.

If you feel strongly that the book you wrote achieves the vision you set out with, then you are probably best off doing nothing. Not all bad reviews are valid. If you think you do need to make changes and can make them at minimal cost, it may be best to do so now, before the book hits the market. If the changes themselves are small but could cost a fair amount due to layout issues, you may opt to make those changes in a revised edition. And on the off chance that the suggested changes are extensive and you agree that these changes are warranted, you will have to weigh the hit to your budget and publication date that making changes would mean against the ill effects of putting out a bad book.

WHEN READERS WON'T BUY IT

Rejection from readers, when no one buys your book, is usually tied to either a lack of solid marketing or bad reviews you have

received after publication. If you feel the problem is with your marketing, try retooling your efforts with the suggestions listed in this chapter and reengaging with your audience. If you received bad reviews, they may have come without warning, or perhaps you knew of problems with the book prior to publication but were unable to do anything about them. In both cases, you are left with the sometimes extraordinary challenge of turning the tide. You do, however, have corrective measures at your disposal.

If the Bad Reviews Were Unfounded

If you received a few bad reviews that seem misplaced or unfounded, you probably don't have much to worry about. If those are the only reviews you've received, however, you will want to tip the scales in your favor by generating as many good reviews as possible. Here's how:

♦ Ask colleagues and business associates to supply reviews on Amazon. Presumably these people would give a favorable assessment of your new book, but you may want to let them know you are looking for honest reviews rather than all five-star reviews. Authentic reviews will go a lot further in correcting a poor image than vague or overblown comments that don't reflect the content of the book.

♦ Approach author-friendly publications to have your book reviewed on their website or in their printed materials. You are trying to outweigh any bad press. That means finding good press, and you do that by asking for it. Newpages.com offers a comprehensive list of review periodicals, but also look to your local media outlets. Blogs are another growing source for book reviews.

♦ Make a major effort to get in front of your readers in person. If you're likeable, potential readers are less likely to believe the bad press. Assuming you can get some good reviews, too, public appearances can win you the undecided vote and generate positive word-of-mouth publicity. Word of mouth continues to be some of the best and most effective publicity you can get. In fact, agent-author Michael Larsen maintains, "Word-of-mouth will make any book succeed, regardless of who publishes it." Your job is to control the message.

If the Bad Reviews Were Warranted

If the reviews you received were a true reflection of the content of the book, you may need to do more than simply engage in an aggressive marketing campaign. You may have to make changes to the book. If you are a self-publisher, consider taking these steps to get your reputation back to where it should be:

- Put out a revised edition. This may be expensive, especially if you are dealing with a printed book and especially if the corrections involve more than just spelling and grammar errors, but it may be your best recourse. Your sales could stall if the issues and errors in your book go unresolved. If that happens, your initial investment in the book may be lost. A further investment may be your only option for making back that money.

- Ask for reviews of the revised edition. Once you have produced the new edition, approach all of the colleagues, friends, and author-friendly publications you can to get new reviews. These reviews may appear on Amazon—certainly helpful—or on a publication's website, on someone's blog, or in print material. Any positive reviews will help. Be sure to spread the word about positive reviews.

- Advertise across all media that a new edition has been published. It is not enough to have good reviews, because, in the cyber age, the bad reviews never go away. You must let the world know that a new and revised edition has been produced.

- ◆ Use the book's front cover to indicate that this is a revised edition. You want to distinguish this book from the one that got panned. Nonfiction writers can include "Revised Edition" on the front cover. Fiction writers may consider a fresh cover design to set the new edition apart.

- ◆ Send the revised edition to the people who gave the first edition a bad review. This may sound scary, but if you can get those original reviewers to acknowledge that the revised edition is much improved, you can consider yourself vindicated. Surely not all reviewers are willing to do you such a favor, but, given the potential impact, it may be worth a try.

Unfortunately, these options may not be available to authors who signed with traditional publishing houses. It is up to the publisher whether or not to produce a revised edition. If your publisher does put out a revised edition, find out what marketing is planned (if any) and determine ways you can complement those efforts. If you can't get the attention of your publisher to do anything about the necessary changes, as a last resort you may decide to find a publisher that will correct the problem. Most publishing contracts include a clause that if the publisher fails to sell a certain number of books two years in a row, the rights revert to the author. You are then free to publish the book yourself or shop it around to other publishers. You may also be able to buy back the rights. It's a sticky situation that you will want to avoid if at all possible, but one that highlights the importance of striving for the highest quality from the beginning.

- - - - - -

Publishing a book is a long journey, and you are bound to be faced with rejection at one point or another along that road. You can do your best work and you will still find people who don't like it. It is up to you as to how you will respond. Honing your writing skills and employing professionalism, persistence, and knowledge

of the market to create a high-quality product are important steps in the right direction. Effective marketing is another key to not only avoiding and recovering from rejection but also finding the success you have been working for. In the end, your attitude and your commitment to the project will be the biggest factors in how you handle rejection and how you choose to move forward.

Mapping Out Your Road to Success

Employ traditional, in-person, and online marketing strategies to ensure your greatest visibility.

Come up with a hook, research the right contacts, and follow up to get the media attention you want.

Launch an author website or blog to use as the hub of your online marketing efforts.

When faced with rejection, create an action plan to move forward.

Last Words

The ideas I have presented in this book are based on two complementary mantras that should guide any author seeking publication. One, publishing a book that sells takes more than just good writing; it also requires market savvy, professionalism, and drive. And two, knowing what to expect and what is expected of you will save you time, money, and embarrassment throughout the publishing endeavor.

By reading this book, you have taken a huge step in setting yourself up for success. You are now aware of the most common potholes that lurk just around the bend, waiting to send you off the road to publication. Now that you know those obstacles are there, you can deftly maneuver around them. Start by creating a business plan to give your project direction. That includes researching the competition, crafting a killer marketing hook, and defining your audience, three important aspects of good writing that too many authors skip. Then insist on professional editing and design. These elements together are key to creating a high-quality, highly marketable book. Without them you are headed for the guardrail.

Once you have the big-picture pieces fitted together, the details demand your attention. This is where aspiring authors can really set themselves apart. Be careful in your research and be thorough in your revisions. Seek permission early for any excerpts you wish to use, understand how to use design effectively, and review your page proofs like a pro. These simple steps will help you to avoid retracing your steps, reworking your manuscript, or allowing devastating errors to find their way into the final book.

For many writers, simply getting over their fears is a major obstacle to publication. Agents are intimidating, editors are mystifying, and designers are a complete unknown. These feelings of uncertainty can be eased when you learn which publishing professionals you will be working with, what you can expect from them, and what they are looking for from you. The recurring theme from the professionals you met in this book is that for them to do their jobs well, they need the trust and respect of the author. Further, open lines of communication, plus a little patience and humility on your part, will improve all of your working relationships—and that leads to a better end result. You are able to do your best work when you are not second-guessing your editor or designer at every turn, and when they see that you trust them to make sound decisions for your book, they are motivated to do so. Together you can create the best, most marketable book possible.

As you work toward creating your high-quality book, whether you are being published traditionally or have taken on the task yourself, you need to let the world know it's coming. That's when you start building buzz. When your book finally arrives, shout it from the rooftops. Then prepare yourself for the long haul. Marketing is likely the hardest part of publishing, and it's something every author must take part in. Once again, it can be intimidating, but thorough preparation will remove enough of that fear to let you make your first moves. Once you get going, build on your momentum by taking every reasonable opportunity to promote yourself and your book. You know how much time and effort it took to make your book; it's time to move beyond your fear of rejection so that you can share it with your readers.

That said, no matter how prepared you are, you will get knocked down at least once as your manuscript makes its transformation into a book. It is up to you as to how you respond to these challenges. If you are serious about having your work published, you must persevere. Call in favors, rely on professionals, and develop a thick skin to get you through. Because although it is a long and trying process to not only write but also publish and sell a book, it is well worth it. There is a reason why people have been writing books for as long as they have. In the end, the reward makes up for all the trials, and you might just find after you see your precious baby in its final form that you're ready to do it all over again.

Resources

BOOKS

The Chicago Manual of Style, 16th ed. This hefty guide is used by nearly all trade and academic book editors for questions on style and bookmaking. See particularly Chapter 4 for information on copyright and securing permissions.

The Complete Guide to Self-Publishing: Everything You Need to Know to Write, Publish, Promote, and Sell Your Own Book, by Marilyn Ross and Sue Collier. Get the ins and outs of self-publishing, including great information on setting up a publishing company.

Developmental Editing: A Handbook for Freelancers, Authors, and Publishers, by Scott Norton. This how-to book is most relevant for freelance editors, but authors will benefit from knowing what their editors are looking for, and Norton's solutions to common problems are most valuable.

Editors on Editing, 3rd ed., edited by Gerald Gross. A compilation of roughly forty essays from some of the biggest names in editing, this book offers an inside look at acquisitions editors, what they do, and how they think.

The Elements of Style, 4th ed., by William Strunk Jr. and E. B. White. This nifty little guide is a good starting point for learning clear and concise writing.

The Elephants of Style, by Bill Walsh. This is an easy-to-use, entertaining style guide from a *Washington Post* copyeditor.

The Essential Guide to Getting Your Book Published: How to Write It, Sell It, and Market It . . . Successfully, by Arielle Eckstut and

David Henry Sterry. This comprehensive guide covers nearly every aspect of book publishing.

How to Sell, Then Write Your Nonfiction Book, by Blythe Camenson. This entry-level book gives a good overview of the proposal process for nonfiction writers. Camenson offers advice for approaching agents as well as publishing houses.

How to Write a Book Proposal, by Michael Larsen. As the title states, this book offers best practices for writing a book proposal from a respected name in the field. If you want an agent, this book is for you.

How to Write a Nonfiction Book: From Planning to Promotion in 6 Simple Steps, by Bobbi Linkemer. This book, aimed at self-publishers, provides prewriting, writing, publishing, and marketing guidance from a forty-year writing veteran.

Mega Book Publicity: 5 Steps to Getting Free Media Exposure for Your Books, by Bob Baker. This brief e-book is packed with great advice on how to contact the media in a way that will get a response.

MLA Style Manual and Guide to Scholarly Publishing, 3rd ed. This style guide from the Modern Language Association is popular with university presses and covers all of the essential points of style.

Thinking Like Your Editor: How to Write Great Serious Nonfiction —and Get It Published, by Susan Rabiner and Alfred Fortunato. If you want to know more about what acquisitions editors are looking for, what they do, and how to have a good working relationship with yours, this book is for you.

WEBSITES

AgentQuery.com (www.agentquery.com). This site offers a huge searchable database of literary agents, complete with contact information, whether the agent is accepting queries, and insights into what the agent is looking for.

Amazon Top Reviewers (www.amazon.com/review/top-reviewers). Find reviewers for your book on Amazon. Top Reviewers are those who have reviewed hundreds if not thousands of books and had their reviews marked "helpful."

Blogger (www.blogger.com). Blogger is a free blog-hosting site from Google. All you need is a Google account to get started.

The Book Designer (www.thebookdesigner.com). Joel Friedlander provides exhaustive resources for self-publishers to help them create, market, and sell high-quality books.

Book Industry Study Group (www.bisg.org). Find the list of BISAC subject headings to determine where your book would be shelved in a bookstore.

BookBaby (www.bookbaby.com). This company offers e-book conversion, distribution, print-on-demand, and other publishing services.

Books in Print (www.booksinprint.com). Use this comprehensive list of books from Bowker to search for competing and comparable titles. You will need a subscription to access it.

CreateSpace (www.createspace.com). This is a division of Amazon.com that offers print-on-demand services.

HiWrite.com (www.hiwrite.com/pro.html). Presented by William Cane, this website offers extensive information on preparing proposals and query letters.

Ingram Content Marketing (www.ingramcontent.com) and its indie-pub sibling IngramSpark (www.ingramspark.com). These two companies provide distribution, print-on-demand, and e-book services for publishers of all sizes.

Jane Friedman: Writing, Reading, and Publishing in the Digital Age (www.janefriedman.com). This blog from publishing veteran Jane Friedman offers excellent information on how to market your book successfully.

Kindle Direct Publishing (https://kdp.amazon.com). KDP offers e-book publishing for Kindle, from Amazon.

Kirkus (www.kirkusreviews.com). This renowned book review service charges a fee for reviews of books submitted by an author. Publishers can submit books without charge, provided the author was not monetarily involved in the publication of the book.

Kobo (www.kobo.com). Kobo sells e-readers and e-books and offers e-book distribution. Find information on Kobo Writing Life and Kobo Publisher Operations via the links at the bottom of the page.

Library of Congress (www.loc.gov). Visit this site for information on Cataloging-in-Publication data and for your Library of Congress Control Number (LCCN).

Literary Market Place (www.literarymarketplace.com). _LMP_ is the traditional source for finding agents and other publishing professionals. The searchable database includes full profiles but requires a subscription. (The limited free database is not worth the time.) You can also get _LMP_ in print.

Lulu (www.lulu.com). This independent company offers print-on-demand and e-book services.

Midwest Book Review (www.midwestbookreview.com). _MBR_ publishes nine magazines of book reviews, each with a different focus. You can have your published print book reviewed for free or pay a small fee for a review of your manuscript, page proofs, advance reader copy (ARC), or e-book.

Nelson Literary Agency (www.nelsonagency.com). Access a range of sample query letters for fiction, along with analyses of why they work.

NewPages (www.newpages.com). This website links to literary magazines, book publishers, newsweeklies, calls for submission, and more.

Nook Press (www.nookpress.com). Create and sell your e-book through Nook Press, a subsidiary of Barnes and Noble.

The Permissions Group (www.permissionsgroup.com). This is a paid service to help you in determining whether excerpts require permission.

The POP Newsletter (www.thepopnewsletter.com). At the blog home for POP Editorial Services, you can find industry news, writing and editing tips, and more resources for authors and editors.

Preditors and Editors (www.pred-ed.com). Search this site for information about any publishing services you are interested in. Brief descriptions include whether the company is not recommended and why.

Publishers Marketplace (www.publishersmarketplace.com). This site provides free information on agents and publishers, what they are looking for, and how to contact them.

Self-Publishing Review (www.selfpublishingreview.com). Dedicated to self-publishing, this site offers reviews and news, plus some publishing services. There is a fee for receiving a review.

Smashwords (www.smashwords.com). This company offers e-book conversion and distribution and has loads of helpful resources.

US Copyright Office (www.copyright.gov). Copyright.gov is an easy-to-read website that answers all of your copyright questions. Go here to register the copyright for your book.

WordPress (www.wordpress.com). Set up a free blog with this blog-hosting site.

Writer's Market (www.writersmarket.com). This is the go-to source for information on publishers. For a small fee you can search its database to find detailed information about thousands of publishers.

ORGANIZATIONS

Association of Authors' Representatives (www.aaronline.org). This trade group for literary agents has a searchable database. You can find agents listings or determine if the agent you are interested in is a member.

Association of Publishers for Special Sales (www.spannet.org). Formerly the Small Publishers Association of America, this organization caters to independent publishers, helping them get their books sold through non-bookstore locations.

Editorial Freelancers Association (www.the-efa.org). This national association of freelancers provides a rate chart for various publishing freelancers as well as a searchable database of freelance editors and other publishing professionals.

Independent Book Publishers Association (www.ibpa-online.org). The IBPA offers resources for independent publishers of all sizes. Membership includes opportunities for discounts and joint marketing.

Science Fiction and Fantasy Writers of America (www.sfwa.org). This organization is an excellent source of information to guide you in all publishing decisions. See especially the *Writer Beware* blog and information on print-on-demand services.

SOCIAL MEDIA SITES TO EXPLORE

Find the sites you enjoy the most to connect with your readers.

Facebook (www.facebook.com). The biggest of the social networks, there is a group for every interest.

Flickr (www.flickr.com). A website dedicated to sharing photos.

Goodreads (www.goodreads.com). A place to rate, share, and discuss books with readers and writers.

Google+ (www.google.com). Google's social media site.

Instagram (www.instagram.com). An app for sharing photos, this site is growing in popularity with teens.

LinkedIn (www.linkedin.com). A business-centric social media site.

Pinterest (www.pinterest.com). A virtual pin board for discovering new ideas.

Reddit (www.reddit.com). A giant virtual bulletin board where you can join conversations on any topic.

Tumblr (www.tumblr.com). A blog-hosting site that specializes in photos and videos.

Twitter (www.twitter.com). A constant stream of 140-character posts, with images and links.

Wattpad (www.wattpad.com). A place to read or post chapters from books in progress and interact with readers, publishers, and other writers.

YouTube (www.youtube.com). Thousands upon thousands of videos.

Acknowledgments

I often wondered why acknowledgments pages were so long, even for the shortest of books. Now I know.

My thanks go first to the professionals featured in this book. The insights and advice they shared have made this book far better than I ever could have made it alone: Emily Ayala, the first self-publisher I ever edited; Bob Baker, who has done such a superb job leading the St. Louis Publishers Association; Denise Betts Frank, my first mentor in the publishing industry; Kathy Clayton, of Greenbelt Editorial Services, a dear friend and colleague; Mich Hancock at 100th Monkey Media; Blythe Hurley, another early mentor and dear friend; Tim Hill, a former workshop attendee and current self-publishing success story; Sue Knopf at Graffolio; Judy Lewin, who shared her story at the first "Sell Your Book!" workshop I held; Kristina Blank Makansi, who stepped up when I really needed her; Angela Ruzicka, another early self-publishing client; and Davis Scott, who has always been happy to help.

Many thanks to my copyeditor and longtime friend Susan Moore; my designer, Sue Hartman; and my proofreader, Sharon Honaker, for their outstanding work on this book. These pros know how to make a writer look good.

A heartfelt thank-you to John Goshorn and Tyler Johnson, who reviewed an early version of this book and offered both encouragement and constructive feedback. Thanks to Alix Moore, who tore my first attempt down and told me to try again. I said she was brutal, but I meant it in the best way possible.

I learned much of what I know about self-publishing and book marketing from the great people at the St. Louis Publishers Association (www.stlouispublishers.org), particularly Bobbi Linkemer, Bob Baker, Maria Rodgers-O'Rourke, Linda Austin, and Kim Wolterman, but many others as well. The SLPA is a terrific resource for any writer or self-publisher largely because of its dedicated members.

My knowledge of bookmaking is founded on the principles I was taught by my editing family at McGraw-Hill. To Gigi Grajdura, Julia Anderson Bauer, Craig Bolt, Nancy Hall, Kristen Eberhard, Heidi Bresnahan, Marisa L'Heureux, and others already mentioned here: I wouldn't be the editor I am if not for your guidance. Thank you.

Thanks also to my family and friends for supporting me, especially my sister Ginny Hinkebein, whose kind words of encouragement stayed with me throughout the long process of writing and publishing this book. If she's right, this book will be flying off the shelves.

And to Chris Pickett, my handsome and strong husband. I love you. I couldn't, and wouldn't, have done it without you.

AN INVITATION

One of my greatest joys is hearing the successes of my clients and readers. Please share your story with me by e-mailing me at books@hoponpublishing.com. Visit my blog for more thoughts and advice on book publishing, and be sure to leave a review of _Perfect Bound_ with your favorite book retailer. Happy writing!

Index

About the Author

Katherine Pickett is the owner of POP Editorial Services and a full-time freelance copyeditor, proofreader, and developmental editor. She has been involved in the publishing industry since 1999, including five years as an in-house production editor with McGraw-Hill Professional, publisher of nonfiction trade books, and two years with the medical textbook publisher Elsevier Inc. She is also a polished speaker and workshop leader.

Since 2009 she has published four personal essays, including "Dented," which was published by *Lowestoft Chronicle* and selected for its 2010 print anthology. Her blog, *The POP Newsletter*, can be found at www.thepopnewsletter.com. She lives in Silver Spring, Maryland, with her husband, Chris, and their daughter, Nancy.

CPSIA information can be obtained at www.ICGtesting.com
Printed in the USA
BVOW07s0538250814

364111BV00001B/8/P